Houseboats, Drugs, Government and the 4th Estate

by

T. J. Nelsen

DORRANCE
PUBLISHING CO
EST. 1920
PITTSBURGH, PENNSYLVANIA 15238

The contents of this work, including, but not limited to, the accuracy of events, people, and places depicted; opinions expressed; permission to use previously published materials included; and any advice given or actions advocated are solely the responsibility of the author, who assumes all liability for said work and indemnifies the publisher against any claims stemming from publication of the work.

Dorrance Publishing Co
585 Alpha Drive Suite 103
Pittsburgh, PA 15238
Visit our website at *www.dorrancebookstore.com*

ISBN: 978-1-4809-1103-1
eISBN: 978-1-4809-1425-4

Contents

Chapter 1   Introductions 1
Chapter 2   Warm Up 11
Chapter 3   Contact 17
Chapter 4   Commitment and Engagement.....................................20
Chapter 5   D. J. Arques 26
Chapter 6   Hands On 30
Chapter 7   Waterworks 37
Chapter 8   Self-Help 43
Chapter 9   The Planning Process...55
Chapter 10   It Starts 63
Chapter 11   December 12, 1977...80
Chapter 12   A Break 92
Chapter 13   Process, Politics, and Review..98
Chapter 14   Consequences...106
Chapter 15   What Now? 118
Conclusion..139
Endnotes...141

Chapter 1

Introductions

This is a story about houseboats, drugs, government, and the 4th Estate. There is also a good bit about me in it, but only because this story is drawn from my experiences, my impressions, and my conclusions. This is not intended to be a complete history of houseboats. The information presented here is not the result of research, interviews, or a scholarly analysis of data, and I do not suggest it is balanced, complete, or fair to all those involved. It is simply about what I experienced and the way I saw it.

The houseboats at the center of this story are mostly located in the Waldo Point Harbor in Richardson Bay, an unincorporated part of Marin County just north of the Sausalito city line and Clipper Yacht Harbor. Richardson Bay is part of the greater San Francisco Bay and the houseboats at Waldo Point are generally referred to as Sausalito houseboats. The principle government entities involved are the County of Marin, headquartered in the Civic Center in San Rafael, and the San Francisco Bay Conservation and Development Commission, presently located in San Francisco on California Street. Among the many others involved are the Reginald Water Quality Control Board, the California Fish and Game Department, the Corps of Engineers, and even the Department of the Interior. The drugs referred to are grass, LSD, peyote, heroin, cocaine, speed, the variations of each, and others, no doubt, of which I've not heard. The 4th Estate comes into it because we have always been colorful enough to be used as filler material when there isn't something better to report and, more to the point, because events related to the "houseboat war" were, at least in the beginning, usually reported in a manner that helped keep the controversy alive and the fight going.

My involvement began in late November 1959 when I was discharged after 3 years in the Army, having enlisted and been sworn just before my seventeenth birthday. I came to Sausalito to be near my parents who had moved to the Bay Area while I was away and were living in a small apartment at 38 Bulkley Street that had a great view of San Francisco Bay and the city. My first sight of Sausalito was while driving down Alexander Avenue from the Golden Gate Bridge. What I could see of Sausalito and the bay reminded me of pictures I'd seen of seaside towns and ports in the Mediterranean, but it was even more beautiful. I was hooked then and there and still am.

I moved in with my mother and father, whom I'd not seen for almost 2 years, goofed off for a couple of days, and then got a job with the Davey Tree Service doing the last kind of work I'd done before enlisting. Davey covered San Francisco and the peninsula, clearing power lines for PG&E and doing homeowner jobs such as trimming, wrecking, and clearing storm damage. As soon as I had some money in my pocket, (at Christmas I'd spent all my accumulated leave pay, plus what little I'd earned from tree work, on presents for my nephews and nieces), I started searching for a place of my own and ended up renting the ground floor, outboard apartment on one of the two Edwards's barges for $127.50 per month including utilities.

Byron Edwards owned two World War II vintage 110' barges: a two-story ex-barracks barge—where I lived—and a one story covered lighter. Both had been divided into apartments and were beached behind a little shop called Battens & Boards that sold snow and water ski equipment a long block north of downtown Sausalito. Almost next door on the shoreline, between the Edwards barges and the city's launching ramp, was Zack's, a popular restaurant and bar that featured weekly turtle races on its outside deck and was continually announcing over a loud speaker for someone to pick up their hamburger. As defense against the noise we were sometimes compelled to join them.

The apartments on the Edwards barges were mostly occupied by bright, friendly, young people, all of whom had jobs, mostly in San Francisco, and a number of slightly older residents from England through Canada, who introduced me to gin and tonic, their favorite libation. We had some great impromptu parties. Being the youngest of the bunch, I was somewhat in awe of my neighbors, in love with several, and did my best to keep up with them. I learned to sail (sort of), water ski, and Peter Shepard, one of the tight-knit group from England, taught me how to scuba dive.

As soon as I was able, I got another job as an apprentice shipwright at Bob Rich's Associated Dredging Co., which occupied the site and the marine ways of the old Sausalito Ship Building Co., not far north of the Edwards barges. I got the job by dropping in on the superintendent, Charley Burgess, so often that he finally got tired of seeing me and told the foreman to put me to work. My intent was to learn how to build boats so I could build my own, but mostly what the yard did was haul commercial boats and barges for bottom jobs and repairs. As an apprentice shipwright earning two dollars and fifty cents per hour, minus deductions, I was able to pay rent, vehicle expenses, buy food, and save $100 per month.

Joe Pasquinuci was foreman of the yard crew. He must have been in his seventies when I met him, and he was a peach. Joe always wore white carpenter's overalls and cap, was built low to the ground, was strong as an ox, sharp as a tack, a crackerjack mechanic—meaning a master boat builder—and he spoke fluent broken English. He'd come to this country a young man and worked all his life on the waterfront, building and repairing wooden vessels. During our half-hour lunch break—the horn on the Sausalito firehouse would blow at noon in those days—Joe would cross Bridgeway, Sausalito's main street running along the waterfront, and walk up Napa St. to the house he'd built for his family years before. He told us he'd eat lunch, have a glass of wine, and, if we could believe him, which we did, sometimes indulge in a little connubial bliss. He always wore a big smile when he came back from lunch. Not bad for a half-hour lunch break and seventy-plus years old. I used the same time to walk to the Caledonia market on Caledonia St., which was owned and operated by Joe's son, Manuel, where I got a quart of whole milk, a French role, lunchmeat, and a package of butter cookies. Then back to work, wolfing the food as I walked. I was usually so stuffed it hurt. But those were the days, before cholesterol and fat-free food. Not being a complete dunce about the work, having taken shop classes in school and having had some experience, I was able to learn a wide variety of tasks at the hand of an expert.

Before I got the job in the boat yard, while I was still doing tree work, I'd enrolled at San Francisco State College for night classes. I was a high school dropout, but had passed the G.E.D. test while in the army, and because of that and my military service, they took me on probation. I continued night school while working in the boat yard, but it was all interrupted on July 3, 1960 when I broke my left arm in an auto accident, and it got badly infected. I was in isolation for twenty-one days before a combination of antibiotics was found that killed the infection. Between the Associated Dredging Co. and the Shipwright and Joiner's Union 1149, Blue Cross covered me even though, strictly speaking, I hadn't worked quite long enough to qualify. Bless them, it would have been a heck of a debt to pay off.

When I got out of the hospital with my arm in a cast and my hand bent over at a right angle while the rotted area healed, I stayed with my parents until I found a one room upstairs apartment in nearby Tam Valley for fifty dollars per month. Being out of work, I could no longer afford the waterside apartment on the Edwards barge. My state disability insurance paid fifty dollars a week, so I was temporarily retired with income. I continued school, hitchhiking or busing it back and forth to S.F., where I also walked the city and haunted used books stores when I could. On one trip, I found a large leather-bound first edition of Ulysses S. Grant's memoirs, but couldn't afford the fifty-dollar price tag, and they wouldn't take payments. Damn!

The car I'd had the accident in was back in business shortly after I was, and when my North Carolina insurance ran out, I purchased a policy from an agency on Miller Avenue in Mill Valley. Whoops! It was canceled because I was too young for the company I'd been signed up with. I went to another agent, and the same thing happened, except this time the reason given was that they didn't insure people who'd been cancelled by other companies. In both cases the agents surely knew I'd be cancelled, but they went through the motions anyway because they got some kind of sales credit, even though the coverage was refused. Next, I tried AAA and they told me up front that I had to be twenty-five years old before they would insure me. That left assigned risk, which I decided wasn't worth it, so I drove without insurance until my twenty-fifth birthday. At which time I marched back into the AAA office in Greenbrae, also in Marin County, to get my auto insurance. "Sorry, you have to be married too," I was told. At that point, I was pretty tired, so I sat on the agent's desk and expressed the hope that they could work around that rule. I had a signed policy in about ten minutes and have been with them ever since.

* * *

While in my little apartment in Tam Valley, I was awakened late one night by someone knocking on my door. I answered and a young man told me he'd fallen asleep and run into my parked car. I went downstairs to have a look, and there was my green '57 MGA parked where I'd left it, and it looked just fine. "No," he said. "That's my car." He pointed to the ditch alongside the road. "That's yours," he said. Our cars were identical. It also turned out his father owned a body shop. They had my car towed, fixed, and returned, and no reports were made by anyone to anyone. What were the odds? On top of that, he had gone to the trouble of finding me in the middle of the night to tell me what had happened. Extraordinary.

After my left hand and wrist healed sufficiently, I had another operation that involved re-breaking and straightening my hand and fusing my wrist bones to a single arm bone. They were all held together with long, stainless pins inserted down through my knuckles—which were removed after the bones knitted. The other arm bone remained disconnected at the wrist, in effect, floating. I couldn't bend my wrist afterward, but my thumb and first and second fingers worked pretty well. Dr. Douglas Ramsey did the surgery and considering the rot-damaged tissue and the broken bones he had to work with, he did a first-class job.

After my rebuild operation, I learned to water ski and I did a lot of swimming as well, off a big riverboat called *South Shore* that had been converted to a houseboat and was berthed at the northeast corner of the Sausalito Yacht Harbor, behind where the post office used to be on Bridgeway. During the summer, the temperature of the top two or three feet of water in the bay is quite tolerable for swimming. Some of the gang from the Edwards barge had moved to *South Shore*, and it had become our new social center. I periodically messed up my cast, and as it was replaced, I was able to observe the new tissue growing back over exposed bones. Very interesting.

Years later, I was hired to wreck out and remove the eighty-nine-foot-long *South Shore* from the heliport houseboat area, where it had been moved so it wouldn't sink in deep water. I still have some knees and a couple of long timbers from among the materials I saved.

While we were wrecking out *South Shore*, we often ate lunch at the Howard Johnson restaurant, just under and past the Richardson Bay Bridge. Entering the restaurant, I noticed that the young restaurant manager was always sitting at the first booth on the left with a different young lady each time. One day, I asked an older waitress at the counter what the deal was. She was upset with her young manager and replied that "the son of a bitch" had placed an ad for a waitress in the local paper, had hired the first girl he interviewed, and then let the ad run. "He's been getting names and phone numbers ever since," she said. That young fellow gave new meaning to the term field expediency.

* * *

My disability insurance ran out after a year, and my one-year lease on the Tam Valley apartment was also up, so I moved into an even smaller room, with a bathroom down the hall, in the Del Monte Hotel in downtown Sausalito for five dollars a week. I learned later that one key fit all the rooms. There were three cheap hotels in Sausalito at the time: the Del Monte on Bridgeway, roughly across from the downtown park; another on a side street, El Portal, across from the south end of the park, I believe called the Sausalito Hotel; and one on Bridgeway just north of where Fred's restaurant is now. While I was at the Del Monte Hotel, the rent was raised twice, and I ended up paying the princely sum of seven dollars a week. The Del Monte's clientele weren't exactly the up-scale types I'd been privileged to know on the Edwards barges, and I think I was the only one paying rent when the place closed down. It was later gutted—which I got a job helping with—in preparation for turning it into apartments.

My arm was still in a cast when I moved to the Del Monte, so I couldn't go back to work in the boatyard, but I needed a job, so I went up and down the streets in Sausalito, shop to shop, seeking employment of any kind. One of the places I tried was the Lito restaurant, almost next door to the hotel, which was scheduled to be re-opened shortly by two sisters. They rejected my application to be their dishwasher, but the night before they were to open, they grabbed me off the sidewalk and asked me to work the next day— opening day—explaining that the fellow they'd hired couldn't make it. I did so and worked for a week, at which time they let me go, saying I was too slow. Another week passed, and they got me off the sidewalk again and asked me to come back. They'd hired two people in my absence and neither could keep up. I worked for them until my cast came off, and I was able to go back to work in the boatyard.

In my younger youth, I'd worked my way through the fifth, sixth, and seventh grades in my grammar school cafeteria and the eighth, ninth, and tenth grades in high school for free lunches—all the lemon meringue pie I could eat and the right to leave class early before the lunch break. It was a class job for any right thinking kid in those days.

I have fond memories of cafeteria work at Sunset Elementary School in Carmel California—back when Carmel was still a resident-serving town and rentals were cheap enough for a single working mother supporting two children. I recall one time when a co-worker and I were in the main dining room cleaning tables after the other kids had finished lunch, and we got into one of our sloppy-wet washrag fights.

He'd just clobbered me, so I'd wet my rag and let fly. He ducked. A teacher, Miss Jordon, the toughest, meanest, and best teacher in the school—she taught seventh grade and all the kids respected her—had just come in late with a tray of food. My sloppy wet washrag hit her square in the face and dropped onto her tray. You can imagine the silence that followed. She stared at me as I looked around to see who could possibly have done such a dastardly deed, but low and behold, there was no one there but me. She didn't say a word, but turned and walked out, probably so I wouldn't see her laughing at my look of terror. Nothing was ever said of the incident, and I was ever after careful to pick my targets. My coworker was scared, too, but he had a good laugh at my expense.

Miss Jordon's cool wasn't an accident. She'd been teaching a lot of years, so when Mike Korslav, a big, dark-haired son of Russian immigrants, put a papier-mâché dog turd on her desk before she arrived one morning, she just looked at it, picked it up with two fingers, and dropped it into her bottom, right-hand desk drawer. She looked at Mike once and then proceeded with the morning's lesson. A somewhat similar scene happened in one of my favorite movies, *A Christmas Story*. Miss Jordon's response was much more effective than if she'd ranted and raved, and we were all dying to see what else was in that bottom drawer, but no one would dream of violating her territory. Mike Korslav was a buddy, and I stood up for him once when he got gaff because of his Russian ancestry. At the time, Russian-supplied T-34 tanks, MIG-15s, artillery, and small arms were being used against the United Nations and United States by the North Koreans and the Chinese in Korea.

Once again, back in the cafeteria after the kids were gone and the cooks were taking a break, another buddy, Don Petty, and I got into a garbage fight starting in the dishwashing corner of the kitchen. He'd flipped something at me, or visa versa, and the fight was on. We had a full thirty-gallon garbage can for ammunition, and when we were done, the ceiling and walls in our part of the kitchen were dripping with garbage and the floor was covered with it. The cooks came back from their break, saw what was happening and, hopping mad, stopped us. We spent a long time cleaning up the mess, and ourselves, missed the last part of recess, and were late to class. We also got suspended from working in the cafeteria, however, they needed us so the suspension only lasted a week. Later, I got the impression that Don Petty was related to the famous racing family, but never found out for sure.

Besides my cafeteria experience, yard work, delivering the Monterey Peninsula Harold, selling the Pine Cone (a smaller newspaper), and work in the Thrift Food Store, I'd also worked in two busy Carmel restaurants after school and during the summers. Add to that K.P. in the army, and I dare say I was somewhat of an expert dishwasher by the time I went to work for the sisters at the Lito. I knew dishwashing wasn't glamorous or lucrative for a young person like being a busboy or a waiter was, but my arm was still in a cast, and I never had to buy food while I worked there. The chef made me roast beef hamburgers and let me have anything else I wanted, except for his moneymaking homemade pies. The sisters put their foot down on that. In turn, I kept him promptly supplied with whatever he needed. I was also able to work as many hours as I wanted, usually around fifty a week, until the sisters called a halt, fearing they'd get caught and have to pay overtime.

During the period I worked at the Lito, I met more people, mostly good, but also some who lived by lying and cheating. Beautiful places attract money and therefore host a disproportionate number of con artists and predators at all levels of the social structure, so I had the opportunity to learn firsthand what was meant by the term "confidence man." The primary lesson being that you can only be "taken" by someone you trust, so it pays to know the people you deal with—or vote for—which is more difficult. Having recently come from an environment where you had to and could trust the guy next to you, I was, at first, relatively easy pickings. Fortunately I didn't have much to pick. I remember when a group of us new guys in the army finally reached the outfit we'd enlisted for, being told by the sergeant who greeted us that thieves weren't tolerated. If we caught one we were to bring him to the orderly room after we were done with him, and he would be court-martialed as soon as he got out of the hospital. If there were any thieves in our group, they became reformed men that day. We never had any problems of that sort from within our outfit.

During my dishwashing period at the Lito, I also became aware of the wider Sausalito waterfront, including the World War II Marinship area, where an entire shipyard, and ninety-three ships, Liberties, Tankers, Fleet oilers, and nineteen barges, had been built during the period from 1942-1945. At the north end of the late shipyard were the Gate 5 houseboats at Waldo Point.

The first time I saw what I would later call "Main Dock" on Arques's property at Gate 5, named after Gate 5 Road, one of the original five entrances to the old Marinship yard, it was evening and had just turned dark. Low Japanese style lamps had been rigged along each side of the raised 6" x 8" toe rails, which along with the numerous potted plants, made the whole thing seem like a memory I had of a dream sequence from a Fred Astaire movie I'd seen in Grauman's Chinese Theater in L.A. with my parents when I was very young. Main Dock in the dark at Gate 5 was definitely dreamlike and exotic.

Eventually my bones and arm were deemed sufficiently healed, the cast came off, and I went back to my job in the boat yard. It didn't take long though for me to realize that if I ever expected to have my own boat, I'd have to buy it. Working for wages, it was going to take a very long time. Eventually I said my goodbyes and struck out into the wide world of working for myself. It was to be my last job with a paycheck. Another realization that soon hit me was that not having a regular schedule, with a regular paycheck, I had to continually turn down invitations from friends, as I could no longer fit into their routines. It required a conscious and somewhat sad decision to continue on my own.

Tree work was my first try when I left the boat yard. My usual helper was a friend who had a pickup. We took jobs wherever we could. Sometimes after storms, we'd drive around Southern Marin looking for trees or limbs that had blown down and then approach the owners for the job of removing them. Sometimes cranking up a chain saw in a neighborhood with a lot of big trees would attract attention, and we'd get jobs that way. Eventually property managers got wind of us, and we picked up work from them. We also cleared lots for builders on occasion, including poison oak, a nasty job from which I still carry scars on one of my hands where my gloves didn't adequately protect me.

Back when I was sixteen, working for the Smith Tree Service in Carmel, my last job before joining the army, a lot of our work was deadwooding, daylighting, and sculpting for appearance. In Marin, the motivation was primarily the concern for the liability arising out of trees or limbs falling on a neighbor's property. In that line of work, we called ourselves "Tree Services," and except for some of the big outfits, most of our work was done with spurs, climbing ropes, fanos (hand saws), chainsaws, pole pruners, and clippers. Now those doing the same work often call themselves arborists, have chippers to handle the brush, and hydraulic cranes to work with and from. It appears that changing one's name in order to change an image and/or to be able to charge more for a service has become popular with both private industry and government.

Trees are definitely special, but they keep on growing and can be trouble if not managed. Anyone buying a house should be conscious of the trees on the property. They are beautiful, can be a great comfort, and do enhance value, but they can have a dark side when around people and structures.

Besides tree work, I spent an increasing amount of time on the waterfront, picking up jobs wherever I could. One of the first being to wreck out the crews quarters and pilot house on the top deck of *Eight Brothers*, an old wooden, self-propelled freight barge that had been used to transport produce and other products from the delta to the cities of the Bay Area before the bridges were built. It was hauled out on one of the ways in the Arques Johnson Street Shipyard near downtown Sausalito at the time I worked on it. Years later, after *Eight Brothers* had been converted into a three unit houseboat, moved twice, and ended up sunk to the roof line at the end of the Napa

Street pier in Sausalito, I got a call from a realtor with, as he said, an offer I couldn't refuse. He was right, and I bought it "as is," raised it, towed it back to Waldo Point where it was originally berthed after its conversion, and eventually made it my home.

* * *

One of my new acquaintances on the waterfront was Nick Miscovich, a ten percenter whose job was to sell boats, barges, etc., that belonged to Donlon J. Arques (pronounced "R KEZ") on Arques's three waterfront properties. Arques owned the Johnson Street Boatyard, where Pelican Yacht Harbor is now located, a portion of the old Marinship Yard, and thirteen mostly underwater blocks at Waldo Point that were crisscrossed by undeveloped, mostly underwater streets owned by the County of Marin. Waldo Point is a prominent hill at the north end of town that years ago had its "point" chopped off for a railroad and a road and was what gave that area of the waterfront its name. At Waldo Point, there were permanently grounded houseboats called arks, floating houseboats, three grounded ferryboats—one, *Charles Van Damm*, which would become possibly the last intact and floatable wooden ferryboat on the West Coast—wrecks of various kinds, and a number of mostly grounded, old working rigs. The Arques property at Waldo Point was home to the largest concentration of houseboats in the San Francisco Bay Area.

The first thing Nick Miscovich tried to sell me was the barely identifiable deck of a worm-demolished barge or boat at Gate 5, saying I could build a living structure on it—and pay rent to Arques—if I started high enough to be out of the tide range. If I'd gone for it, he would have taken my money with a straight face. I declined, but stuck with Nick because he clearly knew boats and the waterfront and was another fountain of knowledge and remembered history. Nick, I soon found out, also owned and operated a small tug, *Marin*, which was powered by a D-13000 Caterpillar that was started by cranking an attached gas "pony" engine, the exhaust of which warmed the main engine, and then engaged it until it started. Lovely sounds and a reliable engine. Nick towed barges and boats in Richardson Bay by himself, mostly on a single towline. He knew what he was doing.

Nick had started life on the water as one of the boys in San Francisco who rowed people and things back and forth to anchored boats and ships. Later he'd run tugs and fished, including over the Colombia River Bar, and in World War II, he had sailed in the Merchant Marine, been sunk twice, the last time being the only survivor in his lifeboat. Nick was, as they say, salty. I got to work on his tug from time to time, and when he sold it, he gave me several hundreds of dollars worth of shackles, blocks, and other rigging gear he had stowed in the fantail of the tug. By then, I was building a small fixed leads pile driver on an old LCM-6 (56' long surplus steel landing craft), which I'd bought on time from Arques, and I used a lot of the gear that Nick gave me to rig working lines. Nick had suggested that it was time for me to stop learning and start earning. I'd been in the habit of talking my way into a wide variety of waterfront jobs for little or no money just so I could learn. My overhead was small, so I could indulge my curiosity. I discovered one way to learn how to do something was to blunder ahead and wait for word from the critics. There was always someone willing to tell me how I should have done a job after the fact.

Chapter 2

Warm Up

By 1969, when the fecal matter seriously hit the fan over the houseboats at Waldo Point, I had done numerous jobs involving boats and harbors and privately owned waterfront property in Richardson Bay and the Greater Bay Area, and my little pile driver barge was about worn out. The steel at the waterline was so thin, I'd patch holes with a sandwich made of two pieces of plywood and gasket material squeezed together by a bolt run through the hole. I couldn't afford a haul-out and a proper repair job. I'd soon replace the steel barge with slightly smaller wood barge.

I had two diesel-powered work boats, one being *Leilani No. 3*, a forty-five-foot tug built in 1913 and re-powered in 1946 with an H Series Cummins, the other a World War II surplus thirty-six-foot Landing Craft Personnel Large or LCPL with a Grey 671. With Arques's permission, I'd built a small L-shaped pier—positioned mostly where the corner of Gate 6 Road is presently located in front of the entrance to Issaquah Dock, a part of Waldo Point Harbor—using scrounged materials and fourteen piles I'd taken off the Strawberry Peninsula and along the Tiburon shore after a southerly storm. I had learned to tow, had done a lot of small boat salvage, a lot of diving work, demolition work, and had managed houseboats belonging to individuals and for an estate administered by the county coroner. I'd also built a rather large houseboat to order on pontoons for a client, worked on, repaired, and transferred houseboats from one form of floatation to another, and had built ten 32' x 16' x 4' concrete barges on which others could build their own houseboats. I charged $2,200 for my concrete barges, complete with one transverse and one longitudinal blockhead, intermediate beams, a concrete deck (unless otherwise specified), and four access hatches with combings. My profit on each, after all expenses, was $200. I believe mine were the first concrete barges built in the Bay Area since World War II.

In short, I had acquired a lot of experience in things related to local waters and houseboats. I'd had a hand in fighting the fire that largely destroyed the old Madden and Lewis shipyard near downtown Sausalito and was third on the scene at the distillery fire where the Whiskey Springs apartments are now located. Sausalito's fire department was mostly volunteer then, and most volunteers showed up at the fires rather than going to the station house first. I wasn't a fireman, but nobody seemed to mind. Everybody pitched in. Both fires had started late in the day and it was a long night in both cases.

At the distillery fire, I'd started at the north entrance between two large buildings but ended up at the south end helping hose down people who were dashing in and out of the burning warehouse trying to rescue some of the booze. Another hose had been positioned behind us on top of a small concrete structure that appeared to be a pump house or boiler room, and the northwest wind kept knocking their stream—very cold—down on us, so we briefly turned our hose on them to make them stop (they couldn't hear us yelling). Between the smoke and the booze, I'm sure there were a lot of headaches the morning after the fire.

I'd also helped fight five houseboat fires, had dealt with the aftermath of the tidal surges that hit the Bay Area after the Alaskan earthquake in 1964, and had worked on the oil spill in the Oakland Estuary that occurred while a Norwegian ship was being dry-docked after a collision with another ship in the San Francisco Bay. Unwittingly, I rented a houseboat I was managing to two young murderers whom I later testified against in court, and I did some work for the movie company that made the TV series, *Ironside*, starring Raymond Burr. They used the ark, *Omphale*, in their pilot story.

A bunch of us waterfront types also helped Juanita Musson move her restaurant from what is now Harbor Drive, across from Clipper Yacht Harbor's office building, to the ferryboat, *Charles Van Damm*, which resulted in so much free food for me, it became embarrassing. She would see me and loudly pull me to the front of the line, so I ended up going elsewhere to eat. In those days, I spent most of my time at work or in local restaurants.

Juanita was a celebrity in Sausalito, and her restaurant on Harbor Drive was her second or third (or so I was told). The first time I saw her was when I went to eat at her place with a good friend, John Wheelwright, who had helped me with tree work and had introduced me to much of the waterfront. John was a gentle, austere young man from an old and prominent Marin family who made his living mostly as a carpenter. He was also 6'8" tall, and he dressed and looked like a lean Paul Bunyan. We were sitting at one of Jaunita's shared tables, starting to eat our ham and eggs, hash browns, English muffins with marmalade, and coffee—a generous staple at Juanita's—when one of her cats (she was and continued to be known for the animals she allowed lose in her restaurants, like garden-variety cats and dogs, chickens, and sometimes a goat) jumped up and started to nibble at John Wheelwright's breakfast. Being hungry, Johnny took umbrage at the uninvited moocher and gently swept the cat off the table, causing it no real discomfort and certainly no injury. Juanita saw him do it, grabbed a frying pan, and came directly to our table. Her intent was clear, and Johnny stood up and up and up to defend himself. Juanita stopped and leaned back to look him in the face. It was the only time I ever saw her back down from anything. I guess she decided no real harm had been done to her cat.

The first rule in Juanita's restaurant was "eat it or wear it," which must have struck a cord with the eating public because her places were always crowded. After her move north to the Van Damm, there would often be a line outside waiting for breakfast. On Sunday mornings, some were in evening gowns, furs, and tails after a posh all-nighter in San Francisco. I saw them, locals, highway patrol, and Hells Angels sitting together at her big, shared tables, all minding their Ps and Qs. Juanita was the undisputed law in her domain, and nobody wanted to cross her. It was slumming at its finest.

By 1969, I had established my credentials and, I believe, had qualified myself as a credible witness to events that were to follow. I knew the waterfront, my neighbors, and much of our history. What I didn't know much about was government, largely because from a tenants standpoint, neither the city of Sausalito, the County of Marin, nor anyone else—besides occasional saber rattling—seemed to have ever had much interest in what happened on the Arques, Tellis, or Kappas houseboat properties at Waldo Point. An entire community, complete with support facilities, a levy, and a road, had grown over a long period of time under those conditions. For something that was birthed without help or hindrance from government, the houseboat community had become a Bay Area landmark, reported on worldwide, and has evolved into one of the most desirable and expensive places in Marin. How can that be?

The one person from government with whom I'd had any real contact was Tom Brown our county tax assessor. I think I met him at Juanita's. He was also a diver and used to hang around the waterfront, so if you bought or acquired a boat or houseboat, he knew about it, and it was subsequently taxed as personal property. And that was long before we were "legal."

Tom was relatively young, personable, and was straightforward in doing his job. Nobody, to my knowledge, had any problems with that. Taxing personal property was the law. Tom was even-handed in its application, and he was respected for it.

That period on the waterfront was a time of individuals; no mobs, no groupthink, no political correctness, and no fear of what "others" would say. The freedom it represented spelled opportunity for many of us young ones who were learning, trying new things, and getting our feet on the ground, that is, until the area was inundated by flower children, other refugees from the '60s, and the hard drugs and hard attitudes that immediately followed.

After the county landed on us, I learned from conversations with building inspectors and others in county government, that the prevailing perception of our houseboat community was that we were a bunch of "hippies, ne'er-dowells, and hopheads." That was fast becoming true with the influx of our un-invited guests. It was also understandable that someone who hadn't lived here awhile would find it difficult to distinguish between the regular houseboaters and the uninvited who were crashing on the property (there wasn't a whole lot of difference in most dress styles and appearance).

In truth, the core of our community was comprised of a wide range of ages, backgrounds, and livelihoods, including working stiffs like me, who were either learning or already accomplished in the trades; white collar types, mostly working in the city; business men and women; a San Francisco building in-spector; a realtor; some retired people; attorneys; doctors and other medical professionals; a stockbroker; a union musician who worked on cruise ships; teachers; some remittance types; and some real artists.

A common attitude the core community shared, besides a mutual love for the water, was respect for the property owner's right to use and run his property any way he wanted and to charge us for its use, including his right to sell or use the property for something other than houseboats if he chose. In fact, when someone was thinking of buying in, the standard representa-tion was that they could probably figure on a five-year life expectancy for the boat they were looking at, since it would probably take that long for Arques to find a buyer for the property—once he decided to sell out—and for the new owner to get permits for another use. The thinking was that we might become a legal permanent use someday, but more likely, Arques would sell to someone who would want to build a yacht harbor and/or a hotel on the prop-erty. There was constant speculation along those lines and houseboat prices re-flected that. A small houseboat could be purchased for $800 to $1,500, or you could build your own for even less on a surplus landing craft or lifeboat or any-thing else that floated. That was pre-building codes, pre-available insurance, and pre-available financing, that is, before we were "legal." After we did become legal, the first of those small, simple houseboats to sell to a newcomer went for $3500. It was immediately loaded on a truck and went to the dump, and a new concrete barge and house were built to replace it.

The core community accepted the basic fact that it wasn't our property. Just as important, we had a "live and let live" acceptance of each other. I can't remember ever hearing anyone seriously criticizing someone else's houseboat design or someone else's success, or someone's ignorance of the ways of the water or construction techniques, or of how modestly or how grandly someone else lived. There was acknowledgement of the fact that most young people didn't have much money or generally know what they were doing, but would learn, and that older people were entitled to enjoy whatever success they had achieved. Besides, it was nobody else's business! The freedom and attitudes that made Waldo Point so special were fragile, though, being dependent on lots of cheap available space, a permissive land-lord, a distant and disinterested government, and low property values. Those factors all disappeared during the turmoil of the '60s and the population push north from San Francisco.

The conditions that made that time special cannot be artificially dupli-cated because they would lack the elements of chance, risk, spontaneity, and the infinite variable of free choice. The participants would only be actors and window dressing in a display for the amusement of tourists. Waldo Point was for a while, I imagine, like our American frontier, where there was always the safety valve of more space and feelings of shared adventure. When our local population explosion occurred, most of us realized that the good old days were a passing thing, and we accepted the fact that at some point we were going to have to conform to real world standards or get out. By then there were simply too many of us too close together in too big an area not to. The main thing for us was to not lose our boats and to still be able to live at Waldo Point if we could.

The push to "clean up the houseboats" started in earnest in 1968 when the county started taking water samples outside people's houseboats when they flushed their toilets. Many houseboat owners bought and installed chem-ical toilets or devices like the Destroilet that incinerated wastes, thinking that would keep the county off our backs. As tenants, the general belief was that pollution was the county's main concern since, just like yachts and most ships that used San Francisco Bay waters, we had no sewer hookups and everything went straight into the bay. We eventually realized that while we were being sin-gled out as polluters, pollution wasn't the county's principal motivation in going after us, and it wasn't clear what was.

An ad hoc houseboat association formed to attempt to do something about government pressure. At the same time, the tenants in our harbor, except occasionally as individuals, had no dialogue with Arques, our landlord, against whom the real pressure was directed. We were on our own, and strictly speaking, had no standing in the underlying issues of land use.

* * *

Arques had much earlier constructed a deep-pit lift station at the head of Main Dock and another between there and Gate 6 Road. The idea was for those sta-tions to accept waste from the arks along the railroad right-of-way and the houseboats on Main Dock and elsewhere, and then pump it into the Sausalito-Marin City Sanitary District force main on Bridgeway, where it would eventu-ally end up in the bay at the south end of Sausalito (but through official channels). Arques told me he wasn't permitted to hook the houseboats up to the district line, though, because the Marin County planning director at the time told him he had to master plan his entire property first, which Arques had no interest in doing. So, Arques's houseboats kept polluting, even though hooking us up wouldn't have had any effect on future planning debates with the county. Much later, the county took an opposite and more enlightened position with the protestors' boats, and they were allowed to hook up years before their fate was determined in the planning process. George Kappas built a similar lift station for the Gate 6 1/2 houseboats and was also denied its use.

The Sanitary District then followed up with a formal policy of not allowing owner operated lift stations, which always seemed unrealistic to me. Kappas East and West Piers were built while that policy was in effect, and, as consequence, each houseboat owner had to buy a pump that was powerful enough to push wastewater all the way into the force main on Bridgeway. By the time Kappas Gate 6 1/2 pier was re-built and the Waldo Point Harbor piers were built, the policy had changed, and lift stations or booster pumps operated by the property owners were permitted. So, the houseboaters in Waldo Point Harbor, the Tellis marina, and Kappas Gate 6 1/2 got to use lower horsepower and cheaper discharge pumps on their individual boats.

In retrospect, it could be postulated that if pollution from harbor boats or the coverage of bay waters were the government's concern, a simple "stop" would have sufficed. As the situation developed, government's deep involvement and insistence on master planning all the houseboat properties actually facilitated a much-extended bay coverage and greatly delayed sewering the boats. As to the property owners dealing with the utilities and the sanitary district, arrangements could have been made and fees paid. Even insurance and financing would have been possible, because traditional Marine standards instead of land standards could have been the norm, complete with marine surveys. The street problem could have been handled through negotiations and trades, which was eventually done under the present system. Government, instead, by insisting to control the final outcome, stifled and discouraged Arques's ability and interest in conducting his waterfront business in an orderly manner, which contributed to the near-anarchy on the Arques property and the lengthy conflict that followed. On the bright side, government's insistence on master plans and land-based codes is the reason that houseboats are today the permanent use on all three of the major houseboat properties. For that, we thank them.

While we were experiencing pressure from the county over pollution, Sausalito and Mill Valley had only primary and secondary treatment plants, and Sausalito, at least, had to discharge direct sometimes, particularly when overloaded by storm runoff, which was apparently getting into the system.

At one regional Water Quality Control hearing, which included a discussion of houseboats, that point was raised relative to the heat on us, and the response was that Sausalito dumping raw sewage in the bay at the south end of Sausalito wasn't as bad as the houseboats—yachts and ships weren't mentioned—because it went into a fast-moving tidal flow. Normally they tried to discharge only on outgoing tides.

Be that as it may, by the standards of Sausalito, Marin County, and probably everyone else in the Western world, by 1969 we were indeed a mess, an eyesore, a dump, and by golly, our government was going to do something about it, as though we'd just popped up somehow without their knowledge. Many of us could accept what was happening, even looked forward to it, and knew that the next step for us, if we could, was to use the pressure against us to make us legal, thus securing a future for our houseboats.

Chapter 3

Contact

On Friday, January 3, 1969, in response to criticism that a lot of the junk and debris at Waldo Point the county was complaining about was actually on the filled portion of their own county "streets," which ran between the blocks that Arques owned, the county hired a crew from Ghilotti Brothers to clear debris from two of the otherwise unused portions of their streets at Gates 5 and 6. Although there was an angry scramble to remove some personal property stored on county property at Gate 6, helped in part by the clearing crew, the cleaning of the "street" near the grounded ferryboat, Issaquah, was completed without incident, mostly using a skip loader and a dump truck. Then, after a lunch break, the cleaning crew moved south down the dirt road between the arks and the railroad tracks to Gate 5 where the area to be cleared was located roughly east and south of the Addington ark, what later became a Waldo Point Harbor office, and the parking lot for "D," or Liberty Dock.

By then, the alarm had gone out that the "British are coming," and a large group was at the barricades to "protect their homes." Destroying homes was not the objective at all, but no one seemed interested in listening to that, partly with the idea of keeping the county out, period. They had strung a rope across the entrance to the Gate 5 houseboat area and were lined up behind it, ready to lie down in front of the "bulldozers," a favorite pastime everywhere in those days. Nobody, including Arques, had bothered to notify his tenants or others who lived on his property about what was scheduled, or why, or to alert them to remove any personal property they may have had stored on those county streets.

One of the fellows who worked for me left my dock at Gate 6 to join the resistance, and I went after him in hopes of keeping him from getting arrested. That was the start of my direct involvement with politics at Waldo Point.

By the time I got to the site of the action, the sheriff deputies were already there and gearing up and highway patrolmen were arriving. Fighting over a bunch of debris seemed pointless to me, but I also knew that some of those at the barricade relished the idea of a confrontation because it was in line with their attitude toward "the establishment," and besides, in those days, everyone was doing it. I wasn't surprised, but was disappointed, that our neighborhood was being dragged into the craziness of the times. I also didn't want to see a fight, and I didn't want to see my employee and friend dragged off to jail, knowing he would get into it for sure. He was big, strong, soft-spoken, intelligent, usually worked in bare feet, and had a great dog named Brown. And, he was so against anyone telling him how to live, that if the rest of the world wore the hippie uniform, had headbands, went about in bare feet, and smoked dope, he would have worn a Brooks Brothers suit, shined his shoes, and inhaled V8 as a way of telling the rest of the world to stuff it. He was also honest as the day is long, a hard worker, and skilled in many of the mechanical trades. He was a good man.

Dean Jennings, Arques's manager at Waldo Point, was present at the site, as well as Joe Forest, a Marin County deputy county counsel, whom I'd previously met and knew slightly. In the hopes of stopping what was about to happen, I got Dean Jennings aside and asked him to fake a phone call to Arques from the pay phone at the old Mohawk gas station, roughly across the street from us on the corner of Gate 5 Road, and to report back that Don Arques denied the county permission to cross his property to get to their street where the debris was located. In fact, Arques could never be reached except at his pleasure. Dean refused, saying Arques had already given the county written permission to cross his property as needed as part of an agreement with the county to avoid abatement actions against him. It was true. I later saw the agreement.

With a proverbial sinking feeling, I then approached Joe Forest who seemed to be in charge for the county and asked, "What if the debris was brought out to them instead of them going in for it?" Joe remembered me enough to listen, and then probably asked if they, the protestors, would do it, whereupon I walked over and talked to some of the guys behind the rope. They agreed it was a good idea. The deal was struck. The louder backed off, the deputies backed off, the rope came down, and a bunch of us spent the rest of the day hand-carrying all manner of things off the county street and some off Arques's property as well, and piled it all on the railroad tracks across the dirt road from the Gate 5 houseboat entrance. By nightfall, a large, long pile, eight or nine feet high, covered the tracks next to our dirt frontage road (tracks that were still occasionally being used). The county spent the following Monday, I believe, loading and taking it all to the dump.

Moving the stuff had not only been hard work, but personally tiring for me because of all the personalities, egos, and attitudes that needed to be persuaded to work until the job was done. We came out of it appearing to be a relatively serious and cohesive group of residents. That was far from the truth, but it would suffice for the occasion. I felt that if we'd failed to follow through on our end of the deal, not only would we be back where we started, but the dynamics of any future relationship with the county would be slanted to our disadvantage. It didn't help that some of our new residents, most with little or nothing to lose and often with well-to-do parents or someone else they could fall back on, would have liked to go down in flames just to demonstrate how evil the system was. I felt we'd been lucky.

* * *

Some while after the Gate 5 incident, I heard that Arques was considering leasing block 227, where A-Dock is now located, to his manager, Dean Jennings, and Bud Fensler (a great guy) and some of his other well to do long-term tenants, then let the county clear off the rest of his property.

Bud Fensler was a veteran of the Marine Corps in the Pacific in World War II who ran a catering business in San Francisco, and who, if a little bigger, could have passed for Santa Claus. He was a confirmed bachelor living on a large houseboat he had built that had a large bedroom, a tiny kitchen, a large, well-stocked bar, and a pool table. He also drove a Mercedes convertible that nobody messed with because he was so well regarded.

Arques's block 227 arrangement would have excluded most of his tenants, including the ark owners, who couldn't move except at great expense, no matter how good their payment records. Not being personally invited to join this select few and having invested a lot of time and effort in my little Marine business, I wasn't particularly eager to be kicked out just then, so I went to see Arques to discuss the situation at his new office on top of Way No. 3 at Marinship. He'd moved his office there after he traded the Johnson Street yard for a ranch way north of us in Snell Valley. I asked him if the rumor about block 227 was true. Arques said yes, that Bud Fensley was a substantial person, would make a great tenant, and that if the rest of the property was cleared, it would be more valuable for resale. That was his entire position in just about those words. I did a quick burn and told him I didn't think he was being fair to his other tenants, that if a lot of them had stopped paying rent, it was because the place had become a dump, and they didn't think they had a future. I told him that I thought he could get permits to use all of his property for houseboats and make the money for himself instead of selling it and letting someone else profit from its use. I told him that I thought the county would be more than happy to go along with any plan that would bring the property up to code because that would solve their problems as well.

Chapter 4

Commitment and Engagement

Arques's response was: "You do it." That brought me up short. But, being young, ignorant, and bullet proof, I figured, "Why not?" I left our meeting and went back to my 8' x 8' office on the corner of my dock on what is now the corner of Gate 6 Road and typed a short "To whom it may concern" letter for Arques's signature. The gist of the letter being that I was given authority over Arques's Waldo Point property and was acting according to his wishes and on his behalf. Most importantly, though, I insisted, and he agreed, that I had the right to disperse any rents I was able to collect. The lack of such a right, to spend at least some of the money he collected, had hamstrung Dean Jennings, his then manager. Dean not only had to turn over all the rents to Arques but he couldn't even use his 10% because that went toward the purchase of *Eight Brothers*.

The story I heard was that Dean had asked to buy *Eight Brothers* while it was still on the ways at Johnson Street and at the same time offered to manage Arques's Waldo Point property, saying he could guarantee to increase the income to Arques by a certain percent the first year. Arques said yes to both, and Dean raised everybody's rent by that percentage as soon as he took over. Anyway, Dean had none of the operating money necessary to carry out his duties. He couldn't hire someone to clean up around the debris boxes much less order additional boxes or pay for repairs or do anything else on the property for the tenants that cost money without going to Arques, which first required finding him and then convincing him the money should be spent, and then actually getting the money. The condition of the property in 1969 would indicate that operating money was rarely forthcoming.

Arques undercut Dean further by allowing others, like me, to create our own mini empires on the property, which Dean Jennings was responsible for managing. Arques had a tendency to tell whoever was in front of him whatever he thought that person wanted to hear, causing endless confusion (which he probably thoroughly enjoyed). There were five shifting divisions of control on the Waldo Point property by 1969 with only Arques able to make decisions for the whole, and he was never around to deal with day-to-day problems.

In short, no one was in charge or responsible for the property as a whole and what went on was as close to anarchy as anything I've ever seen. It was good for some of us who thrived in such an environment, but bad for Arques, bad for the property, bad for most houseboat owners, and ultimately it proved self-destructive. The same day Arques told me "You do it," or perhaps the next (knowing Arques never stayed around very long), I went back to see him and presented my authorization letter. He read it, cracked a smile, and signed it. That was the entire agreement between us, although he did say I could keep 10% of what I collected, the same deal he had had with Jennings.

The 10% proved a joke since there was never anything left over after expenses. It was July 25, 1969, and I was committing myself to a problem that I probably wouldn't have touched with a ten-foot pole if I'd been older and wiser and known what I was doing. On the positive side, I was used to our little world of chaos and was accustomed to working on the water where conditions can constantly change. I also had a naive belief that reason could overcome any problem between people. Of course that requires mutual good will and ignores the truth that there are always those who, for whatever cause, seek to achieve their objectives without regard to reason, fairness, or who gets hurt in the process, or, that to a true believer, the end always justifies the means. By then we had a lot of people with closed minds on the property, and some in government as well, all of whom were against something. I got clear on that real quick.

With the authorization letter in hand, the first thing I did was go to see Dean Jennings and explain what had transpired. He was not particularly happy about it, but at the same time I got the feeling he was relieved to be out of it. As things stood his ability to deal with problems was in name only and that had to have been frustrating. I have no idea if Arques did Dean the courtesy of calling to tell him he was being relieved. I suspect not. Jennings turned over what he described as the rental accounts to me, which amounted to a single sheet of paper with the handwritten names of, as I recall, eighty-five tenants with monthly berthage rates that ranged from $25 to $125. That was it, no dates, no amounts paid, or balances due, or special arrangements, or policy statements.

In addition to the tenants listed, there were also an unknown number of people living on the land and water portions of Arques's property and the intersecting county "streets" who used Arques facilities without permission. The property question was confusing because neither the thirteen blocks Arques owned or the intersecting county streets were defined by signs, fences, marker buoys, or any other conventional form of delineation. Of the three contiguous houseboat properties at Waldo Point—Arques, Kappas and Tellis—only the Tellis property, a single 240' x 400' block, had been carefully marked by the placement of piles and boats and parking.

The Arques property, an area criss-crossed by county streets, was roughly bordered by Clipper Yacht Harbor to the south, Bridgeway and part of Gate 5 Road to the west, Kappas and Tellis to the north, and on the east side, "somewhere out in the water," between us and the channel that runs on our side of the Strawberry Peninsula. That portion of the waterfront was locally thought of as Arques's property since almost all who used both the Arques property and the intersecting county streets were dependent in varying degrees on Arques for access and utilities and garbage disposal (if they didn't throw it overboard) and parking—the things that could be seen—and dependent as well on the unseen. The facility's continued existence depended on property taxes and attorney's fees being paid. In recognition of that dependence, the core community had always paid rent to Arques whether or not they were sure their boats were actually on the blocks that he owned.

The freeloaders made some excuse not to pay or just dipped into the benefits and ignored those who supported them. The cheaters did so in the name of "nobody can own the water," "human rights over property rights," and so forth. Yet somebody had to pay for the fill they parked on, the docks they walked on, the people who put up the power poles that provided them with electricity, those who supplied the water they drank and bathed with, and those who staffed the offices where they got their welfare checks and their food stamps. I also noticed they were willing to fight to preserve the ownership rights to their cars and boats and were quick to deny the use of those possessions to others, and had no problem charging rent for their houseboats when they opted to be landlords.

The first major step after talking to Dean Jennings was to set up a meeting between Don Arques and our district supervisor at the time, Michael Wornum. The meeting was arranged with the help of a friend, Hugh Lawrence, who also happened to be Michael Wornum's attorney.

Marin County was, and is, divided into five supervisorial districts, our neighborhood being in the third district. Having good communication with your supervisor is the key to resolving most controversial issues in the unincorporated portions of Marin County, and we were controversial from the git-go. Each district supervisor can usually bring enough votes along with him or her because all supervisors rely on the same courtesy when a problem is in their district. There are always exceptions, always politics at work, and sometimes, no doubt, a heavy price is exacted for crucial votes. The advantage in our environment was that the other four supervisors were happy to let Michael Wornum carry the ball. There was no political currency to be gained by the other supervisors from direct involvement in our mess, only enemies and/or blame.

The substance of the meeting between Arques and Wornum was that Arques was assured support in getting a plan approved that would bring his property and the houseboats up to code. Wornum thought it would take six months to get those approvals. He was sort of close, as it took just under sixteen months to get what I called our "pilot plan" all the way through the county and the Bay Conservation and Development Commission (BCDC) and to receive the actual building permits, which I picked up on November 13, 1970. The pilot plan was an essential preliminary to establishing our right to cross the intersecting underwater county streets with our docks, thus insuring our ability to use all of Arques's thirteen blocks, which he insisted on, and which was the only directive I ever received from him regarding planning.

When I submitted the pilot plan it included only the two blocks on the south side of his property and showed a long pier with an "L" pointing north at the outboard end. I called that section of the property the "South 40." The county planners immediate response to the pilot plan was that it stuck out too far into the bay. They came back with a sketch showing two short piers side by side on only the inboard block, which from the their point of view was sufficient to accommodate the Arques houseboats. That would have meant abandoning at least the arks and also the three ferryboats—*Charles Van Damm*, *Issaquah*, and *San Rafael*—which I had no intention of doing. Twenty arks, including the three ferryboats, were part of the later approved master plan for the entire property.

I pointed out to the county planners that their two pier plan for just the inboard block wouldn't work because their own ordinance required a minimum 35' fairway between boats on adjoining piers, and even that wasn't enough to turn many boats into their berths from the fairway. They probably had been thinking in terms of fixed structures and setbacks. They dropped the two-pier suggestion, and we got to use both blocks as submitted, and in the future, they generally deferred to me in specifics involving the water.

When we got our pilot plan approved and the permits issued, I immediately returned to the county with the master plan for the entire property, which was designed to satisfy Arques's requirement to use all of his blocks. The plan was essentially to have five piers, including the existing Main Dock and the already approved South 40 pier, which would use or at least touch all of his thirteen blocks and accounted for the existing arks. I held the three longest piers one hundred fifty feet back from the outboard property line in order to help get the plan approved and justified doing so to Arques by pointing out that someday we might need a wave baffle and room inside for a turning basin, which was a possibility. I often wondered if he believed me or if he understood my real objective and just went along. The unused portion of the four blocks at the outboard end of the property later served to simplify a quid pro quo lease trade for the use of inboard streets where the docks crossed.

After the fact, among other things, I was criticized by the protestors about the traditional docks I had planned. My objective was to satisfy Arques's requirement to use all his property, and traditional docks were also the least expensive way to create access and carry all the utility and fire lines required to serve the planned houseboats' berths. I knew that Arques was big on tradition and big on least expensive. It was also important, to me at least, to keep things as simple and inexpensive as possible since, as the ultimate consumers, all costs would eventually be passed on to us, the boat owners. Most importantly, by keeping it traditional, I avoided a debate with county planners over possible ways to cluster boats closer inshore, which would have defeated Arques's requirement to use all his blocks, would have ended the application process, and with it, our future on the property.

As a personal preference, I've always liked traditional docks because everyone tied up to one gets an equal shot at the water. Clustering boats looks more interesting on paper, but there are winners and losers. Clustering also tends to block off areas of water that otherwise would be available for navigation.

* * *

In 1969, the entire Arques property and all its houseboats were served by only one one and a half inch water meter which meant we had to schedule showers and had minimal fire protection. One of the early things I did when I took over management was to talk to the Marin Municipal Water District and get a second one and a half inch meter for which I had to install a $750 backflow prevention device, because someday we might be pumping sewage on the property. Nothing was said about the existing meter that continued to supply us with water. How waste lines could somehow be mistakenly connected to the water lines and then overcome the pressure and get into the water system was not clear to me, but I was so happy they agreed to give us a second meter without us having an approved master plan and building permits that I bowed and said thank you. Seven hundred fifty dollars, though, was a lot of money then, particularly for our bootstrap operation.

As for fires, someone in the neighborhood was usually home, so they were spotted quickly and either extinguished with a garden hose or were totally involved by the time the fire department arrived. I ran my shallow draft workboat around to Gate 6 1/2 once—the tide was in—and put out a fire using a three-inch centrifugal pump rigged with a fire hose adapter. Unfortunately someone had thrown a burning mattress overboard before I got there, and I picked it up in my prop. Mattress springs are a bear to get out of a prop because the spring steel snaps when cut, and you invariably come up bloody after clearing one.

I also stopped building concrete barges when I took over at Waldo Point, feeling that there would be a clear conflict of interest had I continued. Over time three other builders took up the slack and the increased demand.

Also, over time, I became aware of a personal consequence of being in charge. Waldo Point was no longer as fun or carefree as it had been. I had crossed a line and was no longer just one of the guys with all the ease and familiarity that goes with sharing a common status and also being able to do pretty much as I pleased. By getting myself into a position of pushing what I felt was necessary for all of us, based on the situation, available courses of action and my experience with the place and my neighbors, I found that most personal relationships were altered. Close friends and supporters grew closer, those opposed hardened towards me, and others tended to grow distant or dealt with me in a pragmatic manner relative to my job. It was not comfortable, particularly considering the radically different ideas and attitudes involved. I had to constantly test the worth of my ideas against the opinions of both those who agreed and those who disagreed. As long as most of the honest straight shooters backed me, I figured I was on course and doing the right thing. There were no blinders for me anymore to induce feelings of comfort and well being, though I suppose there is also a kind of freedom one derives from losing false expectations, which is maybe what "growing up" means.

Chapter 5

D. J. Arques

Arques had never been enthralled with government in general or with the city of Sausalito and the County of Marin in particular. He simply wouldn't go to the government to ask permission for anything, particularly what he could or could not do on his own property. As a result, he owned and sat on three major waterfront properties and didn't formally work any of them. The oldest of the three was the boatyard at the foot of Johnson Street in downtown Sausalito. His father, apparently in partnership with a man named Crieton, owned and operated that yard for many years, and young Donlan J. Arques spent a lot of time there as a child (their home was in San Francisco).

When I first saw the Johnson Street yard it looked like a museum. Other than people living in old boats, including a derelict sailing ship, there was no visible activity, although Arques and his wife Verna did keep an office upstairs over the entrance to the yard. As you entered, below and past the office to the left, protected from the northwest wind and rain by a wall and roof, was a setup of old, heavy woodworking machinery. The individual pieces were painted green and run by leather belts off a common overhead shaft, which in turn was rotated by a belt from an electric motor. The woodworking machinery was at the head of a wide marine railway, where wood barges and boats had once been built or repaired. Just past the big ways was a second, narrower ways where the 64' x 28', self-propelled *Eight Brothers* sat on a cradle waiting for Dean Jennings to buy it and for me to be hired to remove the pilot house and crews quarters on the upper deck (a bad mistake), so the rest of it would be easier to waterproof.

There were a lot of stories about Arques. The first I heard was about a car he'd parked by a fire hydrant near his Johnson Street yard which was ticketed numerous times and finally towed and stored in the garage that used to be across from the downtown park on El Portal Street, very near one of the three cheap Sausalito hotels. The matter finally went to court, at which time it was established that the hydrant actually belonged to Arques and was on his property. By then the car had been in storage for so long that all the tires were flat and supposedly the city had to make good, maybe even replacing the car. True? I don't know, except that it's the sort of thing Arques would do. He told me more than once that he'd rather spend money on attorneys than on anything the government wanted him to do. Attorneys, according to him, being the lesser of two evils. I'm sure the only reason he let me take a crack at his problems at Waldo Point was the very real threat of abatement actions against him and the resultant clearing costs that would become a lien on his property if done by the county. Initially he was probably just using me as a delaying action.

The second story I heard about him, this related to pressure by the county regarding his Waldo Point property, probably occurring in 1968, was about the only occasion Arques ever attended a board of supervisors' meeting at the Civic Center in San Rafael. He went with Dave Gold, a San Francisco attorney. At some point during the hearing Dave Gold reportedly turned to Arques and, in a stage whisper, said, "You can't do anything with these people," and they got up and walked out. Then the mountain came to Mohammad in the form of Peter Behr, our third district supervisor at the time. I never personally met Peter Behr, but had the impression he was generally well regarded by his peers in Marin. Physically he reminded me of Clifton Web. He was later elected to the state senate.

According to Arques, Peter Behr came to meet with him in his office on top of the head of Way No. 3 in Marinship. During their conversation, while Peter Behr was trying to talk Arques into taking some action at Waldo Point so the county wouldn't have to, he asked Arques something along the lines of, "What do you want to keep all these welfare bums on your property for anyway?" and Arques replied, as he later told me, "What do you mean welfare bums? You've been on the public dole all your adult life!" That was the last time they saw each other or spoke, and it was the start of serious abatement actions against Arques.

In the meantime, a houseboat ordinance and a marina ordinance were passed in order for the county to have something specific to cite and because some houseboaters had pressed the county to tell them what they were actually in violation of and what they had to do to come up to code. The county had been liberally handing out remove or demolish notices. Mine, dated December 4, 1968, was stapled to my gate.

Arques didn't feel any love either for those who didn't pay rent, although he never told them to their face. He let Mrs. Arques do that when she was in town. After I got involved, he frequently told me to "kick the bums out," which I declined to do, on advice of counsel, because of both the street situation and the possibility of a habitability defense. In other words, the freeloaders could have used the problems they'd helped create as a legal defense for not paying rent. Cute. If either issue was raised it would have posed another threat to our future by exposing the street problem as an avenue for opposition and/or by giving everyone an excuse not to pay rent, which would have denied me the primary source of money to pay the costs of plan approvals and permits.

In any case it would have been impossible to do what Arques wanted since I had no money for the legal actions required to evict. I only initiated one unlawful detainer during the years I was on my own managing the property and that was against a lady on a Landing Craft houseboat in the South 40, clearly on Arques's property. She was dealing heroin out of her boat, but had two young daughters living with her, so I couldn't use self-help. Her "old man" died of a heroin overdose while I was trying to get rid of her. The eviction, all the way to execution of judgment, took eighteen months. Twice she showed up in court stoned to the eyeballs, pleaded hardship, and the judge gave her extensions. The day the sheriff was scheduled to escort her off the property, her father, a dentist from Los Angeles, appeared at my 8' x 8' office at Gate 6, paid the money portion of the judgment, and advised me the boat had been sold. The boat is still on the property in the South 40. As for the lady I was trying to evict—she looked a lot like Sophia Loren in the movies, but was ruthless and very much a queen bee in her circles—she kept hooking, stealing, and dealing until, I was told, she was murdered and dumped on Mount Tamalpais.

At the same time Arques was telling me to "kick the bums out," he would hold court with some of the same people and tell them what they wanted to hear: Why should they pay rent anyway when they were just going to be frozen out? He once did it while I was in his office waiting to talk to him, maybe forgetting I was there. He loved to stir up a fight. He also often told me what I wanted to hear, the difference being I got signatures and/or checks from him, sometimes after many tries and many delays.

The worst delay was in getting his signature on an agreement to pay for his share of the required improvements to Gate 6 Road that serves the Arques, Tellis, and Kappas houseboat properties.

* * *

If anyone is due credit or blame for the existence of the present Richardson Bay Waldo Point houseboat communities, it is George Kappas. If George, an immigrant from Greece, hadn't filled what is now Gate 6 Road so he could get to and use the property he was paying taxes on, as well as filling the adjacent parking area for East and West Piers, neither Kappas East and West Piers, Tellis Yellow Ferry Harbor, Kappas Yacht Harbor, nor A-Dock and Issaquah Docks in the Waldo Point Harbor would exist today; there would be no access and no space for parking. The availability of parking being the final requirement for approval of any project or use on real property in our modem society. Oh, Henry Ford, did you have any idea?

By the time we got into the planning process in 1969, no level of government would have approved that much bay fill, particularly, according to the BCDC, for parking for "residences" on the water. By then most property owners were more interested in yacht harbors anyway, a "water oriented recreational use" for which you *could* fill for parking.

Arques couldn't see spending money on Gate 6 Road and wanted a freebie, calling George Kappas "the Greek grocer." I persisted, and with major help from Hugh Lawrence, Arques paid his share, and Gate 6 Road got graded and paved. Arques once told me I reminded him of a bulldog. It's a good thing my teeth didn't fall out as well as my hair (which was an acceptable trade because I think I was getting an ulcer at the time). Don Arques, the guy whose tenants I was trying to collect rent from in order to get the money necessary to pay the costs of his permits, was a major pain. Don Arques was the reason we were here on his property in the first place, he was the biggest obstacle to us remaining here, and finally, a credit he shares with the current owner, Lew Cook, the reason we are still here.

Chapter 6

Hands On

A number of things required immediate attention when I took over management in 1969. The tenants had to be informed about the changeover and their improved prospects, and I had to start cleaning up the property so they would believe me and hopefully resume paying rent (so I could continue to clean up the property and thereby continue to improve their prospects). From the beginning, it was clear to me that my efforts would have to be self-financing, except for the purchase of machinery that Arques could use later on his other properties. I also had to get plans into the county as soon as possible in order to let them know we were serious and, as I was soon to discover, no pun intended, I had to start dealing with a heroin problem.

I walked the property and talked to each of Arques's tenants, most of whom I had known for some years, explained what was going on, the new procedure for paying rent, etc., and most importantly, told them that Arques was committed to making houseboats legal on his property, that they had a future. As it turned out, that was not entirely true. Arques told me several times as the planning process dragged on, to quit what I was doing, that he wasn't going to go along with it any longer. I would go away and then keep coming back until I found him in the right mood to get whatever I needed from him in order to continue the process. It could be wearing at times.

One of the things that needed doing right away was to measure each tenant's houseboat (with their permission) for the maximum width and maximum length, because that is what you need to know in order for a boat to fit in a berth. Knowing the size of each boat also made it possible for me to institute a new rent formula which more fairly reflected each boat owner's use of the property and more fairly distributed costs.

On the administrative side I got permission to hire Edward B. Beattie, "Uncivil Engineer," whom I had met when he was doing work for Arques, checking out the two sewage lift stations that Arques wasn't permitted to use (except for awhile for *Charles Van Damm*, starting with Juanita). One of Ed's clients had given him a set of business cards bearing the title Uncivil Engineer, which Ed handed out to friends. Ed Beattie was not only a competent engineer, but also an intellectual with an open mind, a veteran of Korea, and a genuine good guy.

For legal counsel there was only one possible choice, Hugh Lawrence, who had come onto my dock one day, introduced himself and who, like Ed Beattie, became a life long-friend, counselor, and teacher.

Hugh G. Lawrence, attorney at law, grew up with the idea that lawyering was a noble profession where one could be relied on to work in the best interest of his clients and where a family attorney was as respected as a family doctor. Hugh loved the law, but I don't think he particularly loved the practice. Partly, I suspect, because he usually ended up getting so involved with his client's problems that he spent a lot more time on them than he was willing to bill for.

With a heavy leavening of charm, wit, and clear knowledge of the subject, and the inevitable politics involved, Hugh could almost always cut to the chase and solve a problem without litigation or the costs of protracted negotiations. He also had a hard side and a quick temper when necessary.

Hugh once told me that every time he did things right, he worked himself out of a job because he was no longer necessary. Yet I've never experienced, nor heard of him, milking the clock. His other clients apparently also held him in high regard because many of them were with him for as long as I've known him or for as long as they lived. Hugh was doing a job for the Sausalito Yacht Harbor owner, Herb Madden Sr., at the time I met him, which spoke to his ability on waterfront property matters and general knowledge of the water.

Hugh had been a flyer near the end of World War II, a cop, an insurance adjuster, and finally went to law school. For a while, I think we were the only two guys on the waterfront with crew cuts. Both Ed Beattie and Hugh Lawrence built houseboats at my old dock, and Hugh lived there until A-Dock was built, at which time we all moved to it. Hugh had also been introduced to and had advised the ad hoc houseboat committee that had tried to deal with the county earlier . I say ad hoc because that's what it was: a temporary group getting together to deal with a specific problem. I don't think anyone at the time wanted to risk creating another layer of "government," particularly comprised of neighbors.

Hugh and I also shared participation in several evening activities, including nailing a giant daisy, the brainchild of another friend, George Giampaoli, on the side of one of the four old wooden Moore dry docks. The dry docks had been acquired and moved from the Oakland Estuary to Richardson Bay and then sunk off downtown Sausalito for or by Red Wise while he was waiting to do something with them, supposedly in South

America. At the time, Red Wise was running the old boat yard where I'd worked earlier. The sheriff of Marin County eventually became receiver of the dry docks, which then became home to a group of anchor-outs who were thereby tenants-at-will of the county—I found that amusing—until the dry docks were finally wrecked out and removed by the county using Housing and Urban Development (HUD) money.

In choosing Hugh Lawrence, with Arques's approval, there was also the small matter of Hugh being Michael Wornum's attorney, and that Hugh, of course (as well as some of the rest of us), had helped Michael in his campaign when he ran for the Third District supervisor's seat. I felt that boded well for Arques and houseboats. It was in fact one of those perfect deals where a savvy attorney had two sophisticated clients with matching interests who benefited by working together, and there was no conflict of interest for Supervisor Wornum since all the county heads wanted it to work.

* * *

On the mean side, I found out what was the single biggest problem on the Arques property. It was heroin. Up to the time I started managing the property, I'd been so busy with my own little business on the water that I'd never really paid much attention to what was going on unless it was work-related or had to do with friends. Looking into the matter, I discovered there were a number of active drug stores, or shooting galleries, on the property and during the next year, I got to know seventy junkies by name and many others by sight who either lived on the property or were regular traffic. Some became my teachers in the ways of the business and the addiction. One young man, an ex-stock broker from San Francisco, said he'd gotten hooked going to a shooting gallery in the Fillmore on his lunch breaks. Pretty soon he couldn't work anymore and migrated to "rent-free" Waldo Point. He bought and sold heroin, and his wife stole and hooked to help support their habits. He said that heroin was better than sex, but by then the whole object was to avoid getting junk sick. Another man in his forty's who owned and lived in a gray step van which was licensed and legal, said he'd been a junkie for at least twenty years and that he had no respect for the younger ones who couldn't keep their acts together. He said he would never think of selling his van or his hubcaps or his rifle to pay for dope and that he supported his habit mostly by taking jobs on commission. He would be told by his fence what specific items were needed for clients, then he would break into places like the Eden Roc apartments, above us on Waldo Point, and steal the items ordered. He said he'd been doing it for many years and had never been arrested. He said he never stayed longer than necessary and never messed up a place. If someone came home while he was in their apartment he'd be innocently surprised and fast talk that his friend "Joe" had told him to come in and wait—or to take whatever he had in his hands—and that he'd just gone into the wrong apartment. Then he would apologize for the mistake and leave as quickly as possible. When I started closing drug stores he left on his own without a hassle.

Another fellow claimed his sister had died of an overdose—probably true—and he would relate that sad story as part of a sympathy trip to borrow money so he could buy heroin for himself. His local nickname was "Jack-the-Fluke."

It is fair to say that by 1969, the Arques property at Waldo Point was Needle Park for Southern Marin. Arques's attitude, the confusing layout of the place, the lack of lighting, and the splintered management had made the property a perfect hidey-hole for junkies and others who wanted to stay out of sight. By contrast, Helen Kappas, George Kappas's daughter, whom I credit with protecting her father's interests and the security of her tenants in difficult times, ran a tight ship. It was hard for anyone to use their houseboat harbor, where the Kappas Yacht Harbor is now located, without her knowing it. The same was true of the Tellis property. Mimi Tellis depended on the income from her harbor for herself and her sons, and she had a nice no-nonsense approach that kept their affairs in order. Helen Kappas and Mimi Tellis were smart, tough ladies whom I was honored to call friends and allies. Had Mrs. Arques run Don's property, I'm sure I would never have been made manager, nor would there be this story to tell, even though the Arques property was more subject to problems given the intersecting "streets."

* * *

At the same time I was trying to get the tenants back on board, discovering the junkie problem, and trying to keep the county happy, it was imperative to start seriously cleaning up the place. I figured if left alone long enough, most people would move out on their own accord in order to avoid stepping in dog poop, broken glass, garbage, trash, nails, and mud. There were also, as the county put it, "numerous occupied hutches and hovels," including a young mother and small child living in a refrigerator carton, as well as storage sheds and lots of plain old junk and debris on the filled portions of the Arques and county properties.

Add wet dreary winters to that, and the place at times could be very depressing. I recall a conversation I had with an unhappy young man on one of those wet, cold, and dreary days, who told me that nothing was going right for him and he didn't know what to do. I pointed out to him that the place was littered with junk wood and suggested he borrow a skillsaw from someone and then cut up and split some of the junk wood for kindling, then bundle it, and sell it door to door to people for use in their wood stoves. It would save them the trouble of scrounging. He looked at me like I was crazy and that ended the conversation. A couple weeks later I saw him, and he had a bounce to his step. He said he'd started a firewood business. I never saw him again at Waldo Point.

There were also numerous occupied buses, campers, and cars on the property, as well as abandoned junkers. The occupants of one bus parked outside the fence by the *Charles Van Damm* parking lot, the only paved spot on the property, had wrapped their feces in newspaper and put the little packages in two fifty-five gallon paper drums they'd scored from the cup factory on Gate 5 Road. By the time I got to them, rain had collapsed the drums, and we had to load it all by hand (with shovels). Each situation required finding the owner, if possible, convincing them that we were under the gun and asking them to cooperate by moving out and then follow up, and finally, clean up behind them. I knew a fellow with a half-ton pick-up converted to a tow truck, who would take the dead vehicles, no questions asked, and some were disposed of that way. Others were moved by the owners, sometimes begrudgingly. Some we towed to Arques's Marinship property, where most eventually became scrap metal.

The lady in the refrigerator carton agreed it was no place for a child, stirred herself, and found something better for them off the property.

We bought a small dump truck with Arques's money—he did like machinery—and made regular runs to the dump. There was almost always a discarded, often wet, mattress available to help top a load to keep loose stuff from blowing out. During the cleanup process, part-time employees, volunteers, and I wrecked out and loaded and hauled away numerous structures that didn't belong. That part was particularly slow because of the need to find and communicate with the owners when required, as well as the need to see that no personal property was lost or taken by accident. We temporarily stored a lot of personal belongings in order to expedite the process.

Our garbage system also needed help. When I took over, there were several debris boxes on the property that were usually overflowing—nobody picked up around them—and garbage and trash was scattered far and wide. The dogs loved it. I cancelled the debris boxes, had long wooden dog-proof bins built, stocked them with individual garbage cans, placed them strategically, and had them monitored daily and often. At the same time, we acquired an old surplus deuce-and-a-half garbage truck—very slow—and later a more modern, faster model—both with Arques's money—so we could pick up our own garbage as needed rather than trying to work on a fixed schedule with the big debris boxes. Having no other customers, our guys took the time to clean up as they went. I discovered for myself the well-known fact that when you care enough to keep a place clean and neat, people will generally respect it and cooperate. When a place is a mess, they are just as apt to say "to hell with it" and dump their trash on the ground.

When I told Arques that I intended to run our own garbage service, he said the garbage company would come back at me with an offer of a lower rate, and if I went for it, they would gradually raise it back up to the old price. He also cautioned me against slashed tires, etc., which, according to him, had occurred in the old days when someone tried to compete. Taking no chances, I wrote a polite letter to the garbage company stating that I had no complaint with their service, but that our situation temporarily required an in-house so-lution. Nothing happened to our tires, but they did offer a lower rate.

Some time after we acquired the more modern garbage truck a friend who worked for the Tam Valley Special District approached with a request. I'd met him at Fred's restaurant in Sausalito some years before when he worked for the Sausalito Marin City Sanitary District, and he'd since gone to work for Tam Valley. He had been watching our operation and decided they could run their own garbage service cheaper than contracting out, and they had bought a new truck for that purpose. There was something wrong with their new truck though—I don't remember what— and they needed a temporary back up. No problem. Except, after they'd run ours for a while and had just got their own back on line, our "more modern model" blew its engine. Instead of giving it back in a huff as faulty equipment, they rebuilt the engine in grat-itude for its use, and we ended up with a first class machine for the duration.

I hired Arnie Gross, a recent graduate of Sausalito's New College to be our sanitation engineer. His job was to walk the main dock and various access floats on a poop patrol early each morning before people went to work and again in the afternoon before they came home from work. It made a big dif-ference, and since he knew everybody he was also a goodwill ambassador. I wanted constant visible proof of Arques's commitment. Arnie, being a bright fellow—he was also a contributing writer to our local newspaper, the *Marin Scope*, and wrote some of the most interesting and accurate character profiles I've ever read—made use of his time roaming the property to also collect others' discards, which he then sold at the weekend flea market across the freeway from us in Marin City. Collecting and selling reject items from ar-guably the poorest neighborhood in Marin County became a good and his primary source of income. Go figure.

We ran our own garbage pick up and clean up service until 1977 when the new owner contracted back with Bay Cities Refuse—a good outfit with good people—and our trucks went to Arques's Marinship property or his Snell Valley ranch.

* * *

The county, once we were supplicants, began feeling their oats, and I was re-quired to periodically appear before the board of supervisors to show what I was doing and where we stood in the planning process. They weren't going to let us slide, and they held the continued threat of abatement over our heads. I always appeared with Hugh Lawrence in my corner, figuring that was the best show of seriousness. I also submitted a written status report each time de-tailing progress on planning and clean up. I would list the number of "illegal" structures removed, vehicles towed, cubic yards of debris dumped, and the steps performed in design and planning and submittals and/or scheduled hearings. That went on, I recall, for several months, at which point I said "enough" and simply stopped reporting. Nothing was said by anyone in the county about my failure to appear. I think they were as bored with hearing about us as I was tired of wasting my time preparing reports.

At the outset, I'd established a relationship with the county's lead building inspector for the houseboat area, whose sole responsibility was Waldo Point and houseboats. I spent hours with him in local coffee shops discussing the ways of the world and eventually he saw that we were very much like the human beings in his world, some good and some bad, the principal difference being we lived on the water, sometimes in very small boats. He had a power boat berthed in a San Rafael Yacht Harbor and agreed he could be very comfortable on it only his wife would never go for it. On my side, I learned he had lived a very interesting, although somewhat more structured life, than myself. As a young man, before World War II, he'd learned to fly and had later piloted a glider into Holland during Montgomery's abortive Market Garden offensive. Only a second lieutenant, he said he had briefly ended up in command of the major part of a glider battalion when all the officers senior to him were either dead, incapacitated, or temporarily out of contact. After the war he'd stayed in what was to become the US Air Force and, he said, he had been involved primarily in the construction and operation of airfield control towers. After a career in the military, he went to work for the County of Marin to supplement his retirement income. Dick Larson and I became friends.

Chapter 7

Waterworks

Ever since the Gate 5 debris incident, I had been afraid the county would discover how strong they were and how weak we were. If there'd been a serious confrontation and the county won, which they certainly could have, they would have had no reason to let us try to solve "the houseboat problem" ourselves. In point of numbers, many if not most of the core community would have sat out a confrontation, blaming those who wanted a fight as the cause of our problems in the first place and hoping that somehow those people would be forced to go away and leave us alone (just like we'd prefer the county to leave us alone). People active in county politics who wanted houseboats gone, and there were a lot of them, including our neighbor to the east—the Strawberry Recreation district—would have pushed the county to follow up a victory on the ground with abatement actions, and they might very well have prevailed. Also, at that point, Arques would never go for any deal that only used a piece of his property. By then it was an "all or nothing with him," and since he had no loans on the property, there was nothing anyone could use as leverage to force him to accommodate only his existing tenants. If he couldn't use all his property, he would rather have had bare land and water in one big parcel, which would have been more attractive to sell or trade.

In hopes of avoiding another physical confrontation, I worked out an arrangement with Mr. Larson whereby he would alert me to any immediate problem that had to be solved involving houseboats, in or out of our harbor, so I could take a crack at cooling it before it came to a showdown with the county. One incident—a barge that was beached across the bay from us on the Strawberry Point shoreline to patch wormholes—elicited an alliterative parody on the participants, government, and newspaper reporting:

T. J. Nelsen

Point Counter Point
Strawberry vs. Waldo
Beached Bum is straw that breaks back.
Strawberry residents be-wail bewormed behemoth blocking
Bay beach.
Waldo residents respond, "Bay belongs to boaters!" Bay boaters
blast building blight — say
Strawberry Construction constitutes callous conspicuous
consumption.
Strawberryists say boater's slant slights site's sights of San Francisco
sea scenes!
Rebels rib righteous! Parish posts property! (Nearby Baptist Seminary)
Concerned, cautious county calls for confab to calm countering claims.
Press pans partisan positions to prime passions.

With Mr. Larson's early warnings I was able to diffuse a number of situations that might have escalated and turned out badly for us.

All except, that is, when Mr. Larson was specifically told by Joe Forest, deputy county counsel, not to tell me or Hugh Lawrence that he, Joe Forest, had arranged to have the sheriff seize several boats that were anchored outboard of the Arques property. He'd have some fellow, from the delta I believe, tow them north to the heliport area where they were to be dragged ashore and demolished. Hugh Lawrence and I were waiting at the Civic Center for what we later felt was a deliberately scheduled meeting with Mr. Forest on another matter when the raid took place. As it turned out the whole thing had a keystone cops air about it and only one metal lifeboat/houseboat made it as far as the heliport. The sheriff deputies, fortunately for us, were misused as result of someone's poor understanding of the environment in which they had to operate. Again, we were lucky.

The day after the raid—a Tuesday—was a regularly scheduled, heavily attended meeting of the board of supervisors at which time the board voted for a one-week cooling off period and directed Mr. Larson to prepare and submit a report at the next meeting. Mr. Larson and I met after the hearing, and he was deeply upset. As he saw it, he had been the designated ax-man, and since their plan failed, he was going to be made the goat. Mr. Larson felt betrayed by his superiors and had decided to quit his job and said, "To hell with them." I calmed him down and persuaded him to stay on at least through the next board meeting, telling him I'd do what I could to make things right.

I then put together a large chart, similar to an army training aid, and Fred Jukich, a real artist, boat builder, minor mechanical genius, and adventurer who lived in a beautiful houseboat he'd built and berthed in the Sausalito Yacht Harbor, was kind enough to make me a number of large stamps out of India rubber. I then boldly listed in a vertical column on the left hand side of the chart, all the things we had done in our efforts to clean up the property while we were also working to get permits to bring the houseboats into compliance with county ordinances. Then, using Fred's stamps, I imprinted rows of the appropriate representative symbols in black ink alongside each item on the chart, like swastikas below the canopy of a fighter plane, so everyone could visualize the numbers associated with the actions listed. I wrote a separate statement for Mr. Larson to read. It stated that no houseboater could comply with the houseboat code until the property owners had completed the planning process and there were legal facilities and sewers to connect to, and that he, Dick Larson, recommended a moratorium on enforcement of the houseboat ordinance until the property owners were through the planning process and the facilities were ready to receive the houseboats.

It was not only logical, but got everyone off the hook. The board voted unanimously to accept Mr. Larson's recommendations, and he became the hero of the moment. Instead of trying to explain and justify what had happened with the raid, which was what the board expected, Mr. Larson gained the initiative by changing the terms of the discussion. He offering a solution, and everybody won, but mostly us. Mr. Larson continued to work for the county until he retired for good some years later.

It turned out that the confrontation on the water had been my fault. Earlier I had sent a rather sharply worded letter to Mr. Larson in response to the latest in a series of reports he'd submitted to his superiors that I felt misrepresented both the situation at Waldo Point and our efforts to comply with county mandates. The theme of Mr. Larson's reports had been "Them vs. Us," and it seemed to be setting up justification for a major enforcement move, at least against the Gate 6 area. His immediate boss, Mr. Forest, instead of looking into the points I raised, apparently felt my letter was a personal attack on him, and he decided to up the ante.

Hugh Lawrence later spelled out the whole thing in a letter to the Board of Supervisors, which defused or reversed what up to then had largely been an adversarial relationship.

* * *

From the time Arques said I could try to get permits to use all of his Waldo Point property for houseboats, our small community was never at serious risk of being shut down in the same way that the black community homes and businesses were uprooted in San Francisco by the Western Addition Redevelopment. When the time came for us to come up to code and hook up to the new docks, all we had to do as individual boat owners was install holding tanks and pumps so we could connect to the local sewer system, improve our electrical and gas systems so they were safe, and make sure wood stoves were secure and had ample separation from adjacent combustibles. Many did their own work or hired local help—almost all without permits— were inspected, and were then issued occupancy permits. That was it. Great pains were taken by us and, in turn, by the County of Marin to insure that all boats could comply.

It's true that thereafter we would be compelled to walk on safe, lighted docks, park on pavement, and have hydrants and fire hoses available for fire protection. Tough, I agree, but I figured we could handle it. In the end, when the new docks were finally built and occupied, or rebuilt in the case of Main Dock, we were still the same people, good and bad, in the same beautiful area, joined by newcomers who helped meet the economic requirement for keeping the property for houseboats.

* * *

The moratorium on enforcement, while essential to our survival, was a two edged sword. With the pressure off, I was left alone to deal with the unresolved street problem and all the side effects that had almost brought us down in the first place. Nobody foresaw that the planning process for our master plan, unlike the pilot plan which only took sixteen months, would drag on for several more years. It became a joke among the tenants that when asked I would always tell them that we would be through the planning process "soon." What else could I say?

I continued on what one might call four fronts. First, I had to keep Arques committed. Second, I had to convince the county that we were proceeding diligently. Third, I had to keep the tenants—my friends and neighbors—satisfied with our progress so they would pay their rent. And fourth, I had to continue cleaning up the property, including doing something about the drug problem.

Arques continued to throw me curves. For instance, the very pregnant wife of a flamboyant character went to Arques's office in tears because, she said, they didn't have a place to live. The husband owned two large houseboats, the one they lived on and one under construction. The one they lived on leaked top and bottom because he was too busy creating the second to maintain the first. He didn't pay berthage for either. On the spot, Arques told her they could live on the upper deck of *Charles Van Damm*, which Juanita and her successors had long since vacated. They, of course, entertained their doper friends, who took whatever earlier junkies hadn't already stripped from the boat, including the whistle and other marine gear and any remaining copper pipes (except those that were part of the water service to the top deck) to keep for themselves or to sell for dope money. Arques didn't get a dime for rent or for utilities, which came out of the other tenants pockets, and I couldn't intervene because they were his pets. By contrast, he once made me sign a promissory note for $10,000, which I needed in order to pay some of his property taxes and other bills, saying I should have got the money out of the tenants. I didn't pay him back.

Two of the visitors who were entertained on the *Van Damm* for a short time were Rip Torn and Geraldine Page, whom I've always admired for their talent as actors. He was working on a "Lincoln project." Rip came to me one day for an opinion on a very large, heavily built ship-bowed wooden freight barge berthed near the south end of the Richmond/San Rafael Bridge. Arques's tenant wanted him to invest money in it in order to build a gigantic houseboat to be put at Waldo Point. The barge was very interesting, being one of many unusual vessels produced in the '40s to aid in the war effort. As a potential houseboat, though, it drew too much water to either get to or leave Waldo Point, an un-dredged tidal zone, or as commonly called, a mudflat, except on extreme high tides. In addition, the legal problems they would have had with government alone would probably have required Rip to spend all his money on attorney's fees, because Rip Torn was collectable. His hosts on the *Van Damm*—Arques's "tenants"—had apparently forgotten to check the draft of the barge or mention the legal problems. Rip and Geraldine left shortly thereafter, having become disillusioned, perhaps, with the artistic environment.

During a conversation we had had on the way to or from the barge inspection, Rip accused me of being culturally deprived, even though I did express genuine curiosity about his Lincoln project. I'm afraid he was right. Never having had much interest in fashions or fads, I definitely wasn't in tune with the times, probably the result of two years in a military school when I was very young. We kids had come from far and wide and different backgrounds, but because we wore the same clothes and had the same haircuts and lived in the same circumstances, we grew accustomed to thinking of each other in terms of the person, not appearances (which I'd learned to distrust since they can confuse and sometimes be hard to pierce). Much later, I was blessed with a son who inherited my defects. During an interview to get him into what I thought was a good, private grammar school, he wasn't able to identify the Flintstones whom they deemed a significant part of contemporary culture. We chose a different school.

Much earlier, I had disabled our T.V. at home, so only the V.C.R. worked. For night time entertainment, after homework, our family might read, debate, wrestle (not my wife), play, do art work, or watch movies in a wide range of subjects and languages. I also put a ringbolt through a roof beam and made a trapeze from which my son could swing or spin to his heart's content—that is until he was too tall.

Juanita told me another story about Arques that had occurred while she still occupied the *Van Damm*. She had gotten in trouble with the IRS for not depositing money withheld for taxes and the required employer and employee contributions, so she went to Donny—she called Don Arques Donny— and told him her problem and asked what she should do. He told her not to worry, and she went away. She said she went to him a second time and said, " Donny, Donny, they're going to close me down!" He reassured her again, telling her not to worry, and again she went away. A third time she went to him and cried, "Oh Donny, they closed me down!" He looked her in the eye and said, "Well, we put up a hell of a fight, didn't we?" Vintage Arques.

Keeping the county satisfied was probably my easiest task, largely with Hugh Lawrence's help. For one thing we had direct access to our supervisor,

Michael Wornum, for whom I had great respect. He was an architect by profession, but mostly he was an unflappable Englishman. He could look a riot in the face and not blink nor did he take it too seriously. With him, the sky was never falling. I suspect he was a product of a classical education and had genetically seen it all. He was also, in a respectful manner, very much in charge in his district. As Third District Supervisor, he also sat on the BCDC, the regional agency that had the final word on all San Francisco Bay shoreline projects. We had two other special allies in Marin County government, Margaret Azevedo on the planning commission, a bright wonderful lady, and Allen Bruce, the county administrator who shared many of Michael's traits and kept us on track regarding details and procedures, and to whom I addressed my houseboat status reports. Margaret asked only two conditions of our master plan; to keep a view corridor open between A- and B-Docks and no additional trailers on floats for houseboats. No problem. The other supervisors generally backed Wornum so we had the votes when houseboat matters came before the board.

As for the tenants, I never really kept them happy. None of us were happy about what our neighborhood had become, but I think they knew I was doing what I could on their behalf and the rent money kept coming. The first month after I took over, August 1969, I only collected $300, which didn't pay the water bill. By the time the property changed hands on January 1, 1977, the average monthly rents collected for the year ending December 1976 was $9,395.89. It was clear by then that we were succeeding, and the houseboat owners knew they had a future.

More important than rents was the encouragement and physical support I received from my neighbors during the years we were on our own. Without being asked, there were usually two or three or more men, and sometimes women, who stood witness and/or helped when I closed drug stores. They also provided information and provided, or offered to provide, at personal risk, stakeout locations from where I could observe heroin transactions and use, and I was always backed up if they saw a danger of violence. I couldn't have achieved anything without the backing of our core community, the old timers as we called ourselves, even then. Since I had no money for legal actions, almost everything accomplished on the mixed Arques/county property up to 1977 was done with self-help.

Chapter 8

Self-Help

As conditions had deteriorated in the '60s, some discouraged owners had abandoned their houseboats, usually those grounded boats we called arks that were butted up to the shoreline, close to vehicular activity, noise, and the drug action. Crashers, usually dopers, almost immediately occupied the abandoned boats and that sometimes had a domino effect on adjacent boats. I'm sure the same thing happens with buildings in cities, just as the opposite can occur when people deliberately move into a run down area and start fixing up the place.

The first three boats near the Gate 5 entrance, all small arks, had become crash pads, drug stores, and shooting galleries, and drew a lot of traffic. There was an old tree to the right of the entrance, going in, which we called "dealer tree". In good weather, it was a favorite hangout for junkies waiting to make connections. George Addington's land-bound ark was just inside and to the right of that entrance and the three corner drug stores were ahead and slightly to the left.

The county's narcotics squad, vilified by local human rights champions, was apparently interested at one point. A friend, Steve Warkentin, who had his boat on my dock, went up the hill where the Eden Roc apartments are located on one of his periodic trips to take pictures of our area as it changed over the years and spotted men in civvies looking at the houseboats through binoculars. Steve took their picture. They saw him do it and demanded his camera, but he hung on to it, jumped in his VW bug, and beat it down to my dock with them in hot pursuit. They caught up with Steve on my walkway with his back to my orange gate, ready to fight. Then they identified themselves as police officers and arrested him for interfering. Steve had only one arm, the other being lost in a farming accident when he was a boy. (I wonder how they handcuffed him?) It cost Steve $300 in attorneys fees to get the arrest charges dropped. Bill Stevens, later Judge Stevens, was his attorney. The narks, as they were known, to my knowledge, never busted those three drugstores before my tenure and certainly not during, and Steve, by contrast, had to pay $300 to avoid jail for being curious at the wrong time and place.

Steve owned an old tug, *Pirate*, which had been tastefully converted to a houseboat, was later put on a concrete barge, and can be seen today on B, or Issaquah Dock, the second boat on the right. We used to sit at the small table in its old pilothouse and eat ham hocks and beans and cornbread and drink homebrew, which Steve brewed in the hull in a thirty-gallon plastic garbage can—the good old days. Steve worked for the navy in a management position and was responsible for packaging and shipping bulk materials to Vietnam. Because of the differences in climate and the handling and storage facilities he, on occasion, traveled to the assigned destinations in order to insure the condition of the goods for which he was responsible.

* * *

The three corner drug stores became my first targets. I had already checked out the entire Gate 5 scene to determine the extent of the problem in that area and to identify the participants. George Addington gave me permission to use his ark, which was approximately sixty-eight feet from the closest drug store, for a formal stakeout location to observe the three boats. George was in his eighties and supported himself by collecting and selling scrap metal, old appliances, and anything else of that nature. He had been a tenant of Arques's, who owned the ark George lived in long before I came to Sausalito. Much later, during the houseboat "war," George suffered a stroke, lingered awhile, and died, and I was blamed for creating stress and causing the stroke.

By volunteering his ark as a stakeout location, George Addington put himself at risk, but having lived so close to the action for so long he was eager to help. One of the problems with having a dealer close by, even one who doesn't steal locally, is that his traffic will steal as they come and go—anything that's not nailed down—and George had lost his share. Fortunately, most of what George owned was not very portable, nor easily converted to cash.

I would note here that despite the intensity of the drug traffic on the Arques property, the rest of us were relatively unscathed in proportion to the threat. By then we knew who they were, and they knew we were pissed, and by then, they knew that many of us were also armed, so they tended not to poop on their own doorstep. Of course you couldn't put your tools down and turn your back for more than a couple of minutes, but it could have been worse. One fellow had a box of tools stolen, I think from his house, and the junkie who stole them, who lived next door, forgot where he'd gotten them and tried to sell them back to the fellow from whom he'd stolen them. That didn't go down too well. Most junkies weren't that stupid and didn't want to stir the local waters if they could help it.

After arranging the stakeout location with George, the next step was to set up a meeting with a representative of the county narcotics squad at Hugh Lawrence's office in the 3030 Building near the intersection of Bridgeway and Gate 5 Road, what had been the Marinship Administration Building during World War II. Hugh asked Chief Wright of the Sausalito Police Department to also attend. I wanted a formal meeting because I wanted everything on the record, so to speak, reasoning that if I could figure out what was going on, why couldn't they, and if they knew, why did the problem still exist. The meeting was amicable. I explained what I had discovered and about the offered stake out location from where they could watch heroin being delivered to the three corner arks, listen to conversations, see transactions, and film the participants if they wanted to. Chief Wright was sympathetic, but couldn't take direct action because we were just outside his jurisdiction. He did offer to help in any way he legally could.

Speaking of Chief Wright reminds me of the time I was in Patterson's bar in downtown Sausalito with some friends after a Sausalito City Counsel meeting, which some of us had attended for some reason. I'd gotten into a conversation with Sally Stanford, who was sitting nearby with Chief Wright. I believe Sally was the Vice Mayor of Sausalito at the time. We talked about dogs. She'd had a big white German Shepherd, and I had a black and tan. Her dog had gotten progressively sicker, and she'd taken it to the Veterinary School at Davis hoping for an answer and a cure. She said that the first thing they'd asked her was if her dog wore a flea collar and for how long. Yes he had and for a long time—nothing about brand or type. She said the vet at Davis told her that her Shepherd was suffering from liver failure due to poison absorbed through the skin. It made me think of all the things we put into our stomachs, into our lungs, up our noses, and into our veins, and of all the physiological and psychological consequences we suffer. I took the flea collar off my dog as soon as I got home.

The county narcotics officer at our meeting in Hugh Lawrence's office listened politely to what I had to say, expressed appreciation for the information offered, and agreed the stakeout location was good. He said he would call me in the next day or two to set something up. We parted company, and I waited two or three days and then called him, and he assured me he'd be in touch the next day. I never heard from him, nor spoke to him again, and nothing about the drug scene changed.

My natural paranoia got the best of me then, so I backed off from contact with the sheriff's office because I didn't know who was doing what to whom, and I didn't want any more problems then I already had. Although, I did try every other police agency listed in the phone book, including the FBI, Customs and Border Protection, and the Secret Service. The Secret Service had an office in San Francisco, were listed in the phone book, and answered, "Secret Service." I always thought that was funny because "Where was the secret?" None of those whom I contacted could help because of jurisdiction, and the human damage continued.

The way I saw it, there were several classes of victims to the junk trade. The users were the immediate victims, those who originally had maybe just wanted to get high, or thought it was cool and in conformity with the current fashion in peer pressure, or judged it an expression of rebellion, or maybe had just given up and wanted to go blotto. Most of them rather quickly discovered they were trapped in a cycle of getting high and then trying to find the next hit in order to avoid getting junk sick, where nothing else mattered.

The next class of victims included the user's parents, siblings, loved ones, and anyone else who cared about them. It is not an easy thing to watch the person you love or care for being taken away from you while they are still present to remind you of what they once were. If you've grown up with alcoholic parents or watched someone with Alzheimer's go downhill, you know what I mean. There is also, though sympathy does not come easily here, the young person who is seduced by the promise of easy money and the false respect that goes with being a dealer.

And last, in my opinion, the most far-reaching victim of the drug trade is trust in our system of law and governance, which from the bottom up appears to be either unaware of the realities on the street or to be suffering from corruption somewhere, or worse, is simply not interested; the contract between government and the governed being the most fragile and the most easily damaged, with the most long-lasting consequences. I suppose government's lack of interest is predictable since junkies are not strong advocates for abolition of the drug business, don't represent a voting block, and aren't big contributors to election campaigns.

Between ages seven and nine, I was enrolled in a military school at Lake Elsinore, a little place inland from San Juan Capistrano, while my parents were working out some problems—I don't think I was one of the problems—and there I was taught that when you're in charge you're responsible; there is no excuse. A good philosophy, in my view, particularly as it should apply to those who hold positions of public trust. So there I was, sitting on an intolerable situation with no apparent timely recourse to law, and I could only conclude that if anything was going to be done about heroin at Waldo Point, I would have to do it because I was supposedly in charge and therefore the problem was my responsibility.

Something dramatic and visible was called for right off the bat, so I decided to ambush a Rose cab that I'd watched making heroin deliveries. I got an empty one-gallon Gallo wine bottle and filled it half and half with gasoline and No. 1 Diesel and waited for the cab. I was hoping that a big fire and a crispy critter with some bullet holes in him would be sufficient to get the attention of all concerned. I set it up and waited, but the cab didn't show on its regular schedule, nor did it appear for the next several nights, nor did I ever see it again, nor did I ever again identify a single major delivery source. Although, later, I did become aware of a fellow who seemed to have something to do with a fruit stand in Southern Marin who I'd seen on Gate 5 Road and elsewhere talking to junkies. The fruit business was too neat and well organized for him to be a junkie, if he had anything to do with it, so unless he was doing research or saving souls, I figured he was dealing. His dress and style was also a clue to me as it no doubt was to prospective customers. Taking a chance, I passed on what information I had, along with his license number, to the sheriff's office. I was informed that registration showed the vehicle had just been sold and that no name was on file yet. I got a similar answer to other vehicle inquiries over the years. I was probably just being told it was none of my business. Interestingly, though, the fellow in question dropped out of sight although the fruit stand continued in operation. Whether he got busted or warned off or was working undercover or something else, I never found out.

Sometime after my attempted ambush, an FBI agent, either Robert Goldman or Paul Schumacher came to my dock to show me a picture of an older, bent-nosed fellow and asked if I knew of his whereabouts. It was the driver of the Rose cab.

Was what I intended to do illegal? Yes. If I'd gone through with it and was caught, would I have been tried for murder? Of course. Murder is murder, and valid arguments are made about the dangers and inequities possible when citizens take the law into their own hands. Would my act have been immoral? I don't know. I think the better question is: How long are we willing to watch our children go down the toilet while we wait for someone else to do something?

Heroin and other illegal drugs were involved in or were directly responsible for many deaths in the Waldo Point/Richardson Bay area during the years I'm familiar with. Given that individuals made the free choice to indulge, and ultimately were responsible for their own fate, the absence of those drugs would certainly have resulted in different statistics and a whole lot less heartache for others. Cigarettes and alcohol and cars, spurred by hormones, are dangerous enough. Why add to the mix? To my personal knowledge, three small children drowned as result of stoned parents not paying attention, four people were murdered in drug-related incidents, six (mostly young) people committed suicide, and I don't know precisely how many died of overdoses or prematurely from drug-induced organ failure or lost their teeth and/or appeared to be brain damaged, but the number is significant in all categories.

At the time, it seemed that murders were always reported in the local papers, but suicides weren't usually mentioned, and deaths from overdoses if reported at all were characterized as heart failure or something else. It felt like we'd truly earned ghetto status, being left to stew in our own juices.

A close friend's wife died from heart failure induced by an overdose of cocaine, and he was high as a kite at the funeral, putting the make on his dead wife's sister. At the time, he had no clue he had helped kill his young wife, whom he had re-introduced to cocaine after she had kicked the habit once before. He later lost his houseboat for non-payment of his mortgage and was disbarred for putting his client's money up his nose instead of into their work. He told me he'd been recommended to do a job for a well-known movie director in Hollywood who specialized in gritty off-beat action films, and that when he'd been shown into the director's office, the first thing he saw was a big black marble table with nothing on it except lines of cocaine, just like in the movies. He said that's how he started. It was cool, though, because he was in with the "big boys." Eventually, however, his innate character asserted itself and he thereafter conducted his life in exactly the opposite direction—redemption if I ever saw it.

My experience at Waldo Point since 1969 leads me to the conclusion that people in the dope business are murderers, slow murder perhaps, but murder nonetheless. They murder innocence and human potential and life. I've often wondered what would happen to the drug trade if every parent and sibling and spouse and relative and friend of a victim responded to dope dealers with the same consideration.

Since few people haven't experienced the loss of or damage to a friend or loved one as result of illegal drugs, or know someone who has, I also wonder how many hung juries or innocent verdicts there would be if such matters ended up in court. It is our juries, after all, who in a very personal way, stand in judgment over government's power and can be a very strong expression of citizens' will.

The first time I served on a jury in a criminal matter we were polled as to whether any of us had ever been the victim of a crime, any crime. All who raised their hands were immediately excused. The last time I served, the question was whether any of us had been a victim—or were close to a victim—of just the particular crime being prosecuted. A surprising number raised their hands and then the judge individually questioned each who had responded, and only a few were excused. The message was clear: They might not be able to seat a jury panel in a criminal matter if all victims of crime were excused from the jury duty.

Most of those dealing heroin whom I met, or could identify, were dealing to support their habits, often to each other, so I generally saw them as victims, though the damage they perpetuated was real enough. Since government apparently had no interest in them—except as it related to land use—and wouldn't or couldn't get them off the streets where most of the human damage is done, I figured the best I could hope for was to get them off the property and out of our neighborhood. I never came close to getting all drugs out of Waldo Point Harbor, but we did put a serious dent in at least the heroin traffic and the number of resident junkies by, one way or another, closing thirteen drugstores on the thirty-five acres of private and county land and water that make up our neighborhood. Until, that is, the dopers found shelter under the umbrella of protest politics at the start of the houseboat war in 1977, and the number of guardhouse lawyers increased exponentially.

I had offered law enforcement a unique, one-time opportunity at Waldo Point to corral a significant number of heroin user/dealers. Probably most would not have been jailed, but maybe some could have gotten treatment and maybe kicked the habit, some might have yielded good information, and all would at least have been identified for future reference. Once I started urging them off the property, they scattered, many to San Rafael and West Marin.

Not too long ago, and well after the houseboat "war," the city of Sausalito, in an act of do-gooding (nothing wrong with that), started sending a twelve-passenger Parks and Recreation maxi van to Gate 6 to haul junkies to free lunches—I think in San Rafael—so junkies who didn't already live here were drawn to our neighborhood. Nice. I wondered why Sausalito didn't make their civic center or their downtown park or their library the assembly area. The van stopped coming about the same time there was a group die off from overdoses, probably caused by a better than expected grade of mix.

You can still see the occasional student from Tam or Redwood High come by after school to see if drugs are still available. I once saw three young people shoot up while parked next to trees across the street from A-Dock on Gate 6 Road. I crossed the street and stood in front of their car and wrote down their license number hoping to discourage them from coming back. The best they could do was blink.

We used to have a small garden patio behind the formal landscaping just to the left before you entered A-Dock. A retired high school teacher who owned the first boat on the right almost across from the garden had lovingly built it brick by brick, and when he moved to the Sacramento delta some of our old time dopers, still in business, started using it to work their trade since it was visually secluded, and there was no one immediately available to police it. I removed the outdoor furniture, returned the spot to dirt, and blocked the entrance. A loss to us, but better than the alternative.

* * *

Left on my own with the drug problem at Waldo Point, I approached the individual who appeared to be top dog at each target location, one at a time, and explained that their activity was "uncool and bringing heat on the neighborhood," and that they would have to leave. I usually told them they could have two or three days, at which time I was going to disconnect their utilities and remove their access gangway or ramp and sometimes demolish the structure as well.

Given time to find another place to crash and the fact that none of them wanted official scrutiny—like the police coming to break up a fight that might interfere with both their habits and their business—most moves went smoothly enough (although begrudgingly), and it was all accomplished with only one bloody nose. That occurred when one young man danced around naked while taking pictures of one of the residents helping me who lacked a sense of humor. His son had gotten hooked on dope, so I could understand his anger and frustration. Neighbors standing by with pipe wrenches and wrecking tools on moving day probably helped inspire good behavior.

The bottom line with our junkies, most of whom were in their late teens, twenties, or thirties, white, from middle class backgrounds, and frequently well educated—or should I say, who had had the advantage of being exposed to education—was to do nothing that might interfere with making their next connection. Almost all of the junkies I spoke with at length said they hated the life and wished they had never gotten started. The only thing they liked less was the thought of not getting their next fix. Once addicted, that was all that really mattered in their lives.

I was aware at the time of California tenant/landlord law and knew that evicting the junkies without due process was blatantly illegal, and that Arques could be sued for damages if anyone exercised their rights. However, I correctly judged that no one was interested in getting attorneys or the law involved. The whole thing was done upfront, people to people, and it worked.

I also rigged lights in the darker areas shoreside, which were repeatedly shot out, mostly with a 12-gauge shotgun, and had their electric lines repeatedly cut. Eventually I was able to persuade an acquaintance in the Mill Valley Pacific Gas and Electric office to authorize proper streetlights wherever PG&E had a pole on or near the property, which were also shot out until they switched to bullet-resistant lenses. Hidey-holes lose their value when well lighted, providing there is a follow-up on the ground. I also quickly learned it was necessary to demolish all abandoned or vacated structures, or they would be reoccupied by a new batch of dopers.

One group who fancied themselves "pirates" were a particular problem because of their greater experience and skills. For a while, they ran a small, quiet, Monterey-style boat, painted black, in and out of local harbors at night stealing re-sellable valuables off of yachts. Without running lights they were hard to see. Over time, they lived individually or together in different places on the property, and I had to wreck out two of the structures they occupied. One being another of the 110' x 32' grounded covered lighters that had been turned into a very large houseboat, abandoned by the original owners, and had become known as the Tiltin Hilton. The other being a very old sixty-foot (I believe) grounded tugboat called *Mariner*, both of which were in the South 40. *Mariner* had first been berthed on Main Dock between the ark, *Benicia*, and where Cyra McFadden's houseboat is now located, but was moved to a shallower location in the South 40 by its owner when it became too hard to keep afloat and was later abandoned.

One of the pirate group told me they would sometimes get themselves busted for something minor during the winters just to have a warm, dry place to stay for a while, kind of like in the old O' Henry story, and also to help reduce their habits. Although, he said, they could still get heroin or methadone in jail via visitors. At the same time, simple things like keeping one's household together and supplied with firewood was a major problem for most junkies. The same guy complimented me later for what I had been trying to do and was one of two who were able to eventually clean up their acts and get good jobs and a life. Two committed suicide, and I don't know what became of the rest.

Because I knew most of them, and we had had some kind of relationship before 1969 when I took over management, I was generally able to deal with them one-on-one without help, except for when it came to wrecking. Most didn't like me, but they were bright enough to know that what I was doing was both inevitable, probably the right thing, and that it was better me than the county and the sheriff. I pushed that thought hard.

The process of easing the junkies out wasn't all straightforward. One night, I saw a couple of them on Bridgeway, across from Gate 5, hitchhiking to downtown Sausalito. I waited nearby and when a car stopped for them I jumped in too—to their chagrin—and we chitchatted about drugs, cops, and such like, all the way downtown where we parted company, and I hitched a ride back to Waldo Point. It was sometimes useful to out-crazy the crazies. Also, on occasion, I wasn't completely on the level with them and just did whatever I could to keep them off balance and feeling insecure in our neighborhood, like bursting into one of their crash pads in the middle of the night and saying the sheriff was on his way to make a bust. That was good for scattering some of them for a short while and tended to inhibit drug deliveries and clients for a short while.

I often walked the houseboat area at night to see what was going on and to talk to anyone I happened to meet. It was always enlightening in both regards. My theory was to get as close to a problem as possible, whether government or junkies, both to improve understanding and communication in both directions and to limit the opposition's maneuvering room.

One night, I was approached by one of the older junkies, an ex-marine who had earlier told me that he'd written a book based on his experiences in Korea. He asked me to give him my .38, an ancient Smith and Wesson I'd bought from a friend for fifteen dollars, and that I'd let them know I carried on my rounds at night, so he could sell or trade it for a fix. I said no, but that I'd "loan" him ten dollars—nickel bags in New York at the time and dime bags on the West Coast—if he'd take me with him, the money to be handed over at the dealer's location. He agreed, and I drove him to the Bermuda Palms Motel in San Rafael, where he scored. I wasn't allowed in, but had to wait in a darkened hallway, so I wasn't able to identify anyone. Then I drove him back to Gate 6 where in the dark and wet of an old sunk houseboat—the tide was out—I held the match to help him cook the heroin and he shot up (part of my education). He later killed himself. I kept a small collection of souvenirs from those days, including a substance I believed to be heroin, plus spoons, needles, hypodermics, dried out balloons, and various caliber bullets.

* * *

Well into my cleaning and clearing operation, a gentleman, Robbie Robison, approached me with a proposition. I'd known him since an incident when a young man had come to the waterfront looking for his sister. She was reportedly on Robbie's boat, anchored some distance out from my dock. The brother was concerned about his sister, fearing she might be in the clutches of a "dope crazed hippie," and he wanted me to take him out to Robbie's on my workboat. I agreed on the condition that we'd stand off and hail Robbie, who I didn't know by name at that time, to see what was up. We did so and Robbie, who looked something like a good looking, well groomed Hagar the Horrible, politely responded, called the young lady on deck, and all three of us returned to my dock where they parted as new friends. I was impressed by Robbie's cool and his sense of propriety. At the time, Robbie was taking it easy after riding motorcycles and playing and singing in bands. He'd also done a tour in the air force, where an injury had left him with a wound that wouldn't heal and that years later, would cost him a leg. For now, though, he had a proposition for me. He had been watching my activities and wanted to become my sheriff. Well, I could use the help and respected his communication skills, but to begin with, we just talked. However, Robbie wasn't one to let my reticence slow him down. He applied for and took a training course and received a permit to carry a gun as an armed security guard—he'd brought paperwork for me to sign as his employer and showed up one day wearing a blouse made out of a Levi jacket complete with hand-sewn shoulder patches and a handmade brass sheriff's star—and packing a model 1911 Army Colt .45, ready to go to work. Among his other skills, Robbie was an artist. Robbie also knew everyone in the neighborhood, loved to talk, and was serious about keeping the peace.

Robbie was good at his job, became a primary source of intelligence and, unfortunately for him, became another lightening rod during the nastiness of the houseboat war starting in 1977. During that later period, Robbie absorbed a lot of heat that otherwise would have been directed at me, but he gritted his teeth and never flinched. At the end of the houseboat war, though, he was so embittered by death threats to his wife and small children by people whom he had thought to be his friends, that he refused a berth—which he could have sold—and moved out of the area.

In an open letter to the Houseboat Community, in July of 1977, Robbie expressed his view of what was happening to our community:

ROBBIE ROBISON
P. O. BOX 484   July 28, 1977

An open letter from Robbie Robison

Since the Waldo Point area has not been very peaceful lately, it seems to me I've been flunking as keeper of the peace. I will try to do better in the future. There seems to be reference at this time to a song I wrote several years ago, and the term "Free People" has been used. I'd like to clear up a misunderstanding and give my definition of "Free People," that is "free mooring" or "anchor-out," and the independence referred to being on your own anchor on your own boat in a free anchorage. It never meant that I ever expected or even wanted free berths, free water piped in, free gas, free electricity, free garbage collection or free parking lots, etc. It never meant living so close to shore that

I'd be sitting on the mud flushing my head or pumping my bilge, or my boat's bilge.

When I wrote that song I got the message that the county saw this area—Gates 5 and 6—as a floating hobo jungle, and it would only be a matter of time before it would end. I was there when the county wanted to clean their streets and was aware they had the commitment and the facilities.

Mr. Arques left his keys in the car, and just about everybody I know drove it. Some paid for their own gasoline, but there were others who wouldn't fix a flat if they had one. When the government made the car get a smog device and the proper muffler and registration (come up to code), the car was leased to Mr. Cook and Company. They plan to bring the car up to the legal requirements but no more free keys. . . if you use the car you pay for the trip.

It looks like some want to wreck the car so that no one can drive it because they don't want to drive if it's got a license. If they put as much effort into helping the car become legal as they are into wrecking it, they could probably go along for the ride.

Up till now I've kept my mouth shut because I don't own a houseboat anymore. But all along I've been convinced that the only way to secure a future here in Marin County for houseboats is to acknowledge the county regulations. Without the developer's money to bring the area up to code, they would abate the whole property. Then even if your boat was legal the property wouldn't be, and the county would make you move it. The definition of the word "make" is to force.

The Health Department flunked us, the Fire Department flunked us, our walkways are unsafe, and I have been amazed that this place has made it this long. It's so amazing that some must believe we are immune.

Some fight because they feel committed to a cause, some fight authority, some fight for attention, some fight progress, some fight for acceptance some fight for time, some fight bill collectors, and some just fight—

Those who can sail away are the free people. What of the ones who have to stay and want to stay? After the war is over what do they do?

This opinion was prompted by all the non-houseboat owners who are participating in the demonstrations here, since I can identify with them. We are not houseboat owners, but we seem to be involved anyway.

Robbie Robinson

After Robbie started as sheriff, well before Lew Cook's time, we'd occasionally go together to some local restaurant for lunch, forgetting that the real world was out there and that guys who looked like Robbie didn't ordinarily go out in public packing a .45 on their hip. We had to do some explaining to police in surrounding jurisdictions until they got to know us, and the word went out that Robbie was okay. At the time, it was like there were two very different worlds with different rules existing side by side. Sheath knives were a popular accessory for many on the waterfront, particularly for our local pirate types.

Once I had Robbie sit by the walkway leading to a small houseboat built on a twenty-two-foot lifeboat that had been turned into a drugstore in the Gate 6 area, where he photographed everyone who went into or came out of that boat. No one came the second day, and the guy who had been selling the heroin ended up walking around in the mud near my dock, trying to get in to see me. He could have just walked up to my orange gate and knocked or hollered.

I took him to San Rafael hoping to get him into some kind of treatment or methadone program. After trying three locations—he was dirty and he stank—I left him at the last place telling them he was theirs. Nobody wanted him. It was my impression that their interests were in clean, middle-class kids who needed someone to hold their hands, not hardcore junkies. He got a ride and beat me back to Waldo Point. His twenty-two-foot boat was then taken over by a son of Alan Watts, another local celebrity, and moved to the South 40, where the son in turn set up shop. I told him that was no good, and with the unexpected help of a fellow who's storage shack I'd demolished—I'd first moved his belongings to another location for him—we towed the lifeboat drugstore out of the South 40 and beached it just south of the Arques property next to the ferryboat *Vallejo*, where the young man's father lived. I don't think either father or son appreciated me putting them back together again. The little drugstore was eventually abandoned and destroyed.

Not unexpectedly, there were occasional threats in various forms, but as Robbie was told by one of the dopers, those with the greatest beef against me were usually the least able to do anything about it.

The guys who shot out the lights with a shotgun were an exception to that general rule. Once, just after dark with me standing on my houseboat in plain sight, they took a shot at the light on a PG&E pole located near the foot of my dock at Gate 6. I'd recently accepted the offered loan of a 12 gauge Remington pump, so I took that and checked out the dark area, which is now parking and landscaping for Kappas East and West Piers, but was then covered by mounds of dirt that had been dumped there to be used in raising the grade. I didn't find anyone. They must have come by water all the way around the Tellis and Kappas harbors into the lagoon where East and West Piers are now located, and it didn't occur to me to check the water. If they did come that way, they could probably see me the whole time and got a good chuckle out of it, even though they may not have gotten the reaction they were hoping for.

"Those living outside the law", as Louis L'Amour expressed in his 1964 Western novel, *Hanging Woman Creek*, "always make light of honest men, but what they never seem to realize is that honest men can get mad."

Chapter 9

The Planning Process

The planning process dragged on. Our master plan approval at the county level was relatively quick because everyone wanted to expedite solving the houseboat problem. The big hang up was the BCDC staff. First, for their convenience, they wanted the plans for the Kappas, Arques, and Tellis properties combined into a single, giant master plan. The relationships of the three plans were already clear, the county had no problems with them, and none of the details changed because we'd already coordinated the three plans where they touched at Gate 6 Road. Then the BCDC started whittling away at the plans that had been approved by the county.

The cuts on the Arques plan came along the shoreline areas that provided parking. Helen Kappas, on behalf of her father George, and I went back and forth to the BCDC office in San Francisco, then on Van Ness Avenue, with new drawings after arguing each time for what we had to have. Being new to the system we thought at first that the BCDC staff had some special insight into planning in general and specifically in regards to their duty under the rules laid down by the McAteer-Petris Act which was supposedly their guide in evaluating proposals brought before them. It was nothing of the sort. They would ask for a change, we would agree to what we thought we could live with, and then go home, redraw the plans and return for approval. Woops! Need another change. We finally realized they were stonewalling us and had no intention of forwarding a recommendation for approval to the full commission, regardless of what the rules said. Later, during the houseboat war, the BCDC staff, when it was in their interest to do so, ignored or reversed the positions and the justification they'd used when requiring us to make changes, thus freely exercising their discretion to change their minds to make life easier for themselves or to further their own ends, whatever that happened to mean at the moment.

Time to call in the big guns. A breakfast meeting at a pancake house on Lombard Street was arranged between Al Baum, the BCDC's man whom Helen and I had primarily dealt with, and Michael Wornum who was both our supervisor and BCDC commissioner for Marin County. Hugh Lawrence and I were also present. The meeting was short and to the point and I barely got through a stack of pancakes. Michael Wornum simply told Al Baum that approval of our plan was very important to the County of Marin and ordered him to expedite. When Helen Kappas and I showed up in Mr. Baum's office, I believe the next day, we were told that everything was okay and the staff would recommend approval.

It seems that the BCDC staff felt it was their mission to chisel away or block whatever plan came before them regardless of purpose or suitability or the law. While an applicant's financing, contractual arrangements, and in our case, the residents' futures, hung in the balance; the staffs' discretionary (read extortionary) power is pretty much absolute so long as they sort of stay within the confines of the law under which they operate and which they alone interpret, short of a court order. Legal challenges to their decisions mean very long delays and increased costs. Unless an applicant has a BCDC commissioner in their corner who understands the application and is willing to campaign for votes, the staff, an unelected, unaccountable group of professional bureaucrats, pretty much runs the commission and makes the decisions. Their control is so complete they can ask for contributions to "clean up" funds as a condition for plan approval and call it mitigation, the need for mitigation in the first place being determined by themselves. Obviously, to the BCDC staff, the people who come through their doors as applicants are not only the enemy, but it's okay to pick their pockets.

Next, I spent time with the BCDC design review board, most of which involved the placement and type of plants we were to use for landscaping and the size pots they were to come in, which of course required more drawings. A neighbor, Ron Young, who lived on a houseboat at Kappas Gate 6 1/2 was hired for that purpose.

I've never understood government's consuming interest in the type, size, and number of plants and trees to be planted, the width of paths, or the type and size of benches. There seems to be a built-in presumption that without government's superior guidance, ordinary human beings, the people who live and work in the real world, don't have the intelligence or the incentive to do the "right thing"—to choose for themselves what to plant or where, nor the interest in or knowledge of how to make private property attractive and comfortable for themselves, the use of their tenants, their customers, or the public, or indeed even have the right to do so. One might as well forego wasting one's time and money hiring one's own experts and instead submit a rough sketch on butcher paper and let government redesign everything, since they will try to as a matter of form anyway.

To be fair, however, if you look at all off government's hemming and hawing as a job security program for bureaucrats and professionals and/or as a way for people on the political ladder to be able to put on their resume that they sat on this or that committee as "experts" judging how other people should live and do things, then at least their actions make sense. It particularly makes sense when you remember that the people who invest time and money and effort and create jobs and actually do something are popularly characterized as being evil, while the people who make them jump through hoops are portrayed as good guys whose only interest is our well-being. And if you believe all that, I've got a bridge I'll sell you.

Government is right there when it comes to micromanaging the plans for someone else's property and getting their cut in the process, but when it comes to the down and dirty, important life and death stuff, like getting drug dealers out of a neighborhood, government is somewhere else.

Our next step at the BCDC was its Engineering Review Board. That went pretty quick and was the most down to earth of the three BCDC hurdles at the time. One fellow, though, insisted we couldn't prove that the piling design we'd specified would withstand wind loading so he was blocking approval. I'd done a pile test to at least prove bearing capacity by building a big plywood box around the top of a short, skinny pile, caulking it, and filling it with water. It waved around in the northwest wind for, as I recall, a couple of weeks with a transit monitoring it the whole time, and it did just fine. In response to the gentleman blocking approval, I was about to say something about local experience when Ed Beattie, who was with me, elbowed me in the side to keep me quiet, at which point an engineer who had been silent up until then spoke up. He said that the plan we had presented did indeed represent the state of the art even though it was arguable whether we could justify parts of it mathematically. That ended the discussion and the engineering board rubber-stamped our plan. Ed later told me that our savior had "written the book" on pile driving and was presently teaching.

Earlier, I'd read somewhere that there had been no subaqueous foundation failures on the San Francisco waterfront during the '06 earthquake. There was damage to buildings, but no pile failures. So far, we've been through years of storms plus the 1988 quake with no foundation failures. Knock on wood. Both the BCDC design and engineering review boards were duplications of county functions.

By the end of the application process with the BCDC we had had, I recall, seven hearings for our plans and for necessary amendments before the full BCDC commission. At one hearing, the agenda item ahead of ours was being discussed with the use of large and very clear maps and visual aids. One of the commissioners spoke up to object saying, "How do we know they will really clean it up and keep it clean?" The project before the commission involved a piece of bare shoreline property in San Francisco somewhere near Candlestick Park. Apparently the commissioner had seen the word houseboat on the printed agenda and thought they were talking about us. He was answered with embarrassed silence. That commissioner was part of the reason BCDC staff exercised so much power in determining what got approved and the conditions of approval, instead of the commissioners, who are supposed to be familiar with the issues and responsive to applicants and others through public hearings, making those determinations. We were extremely fortunate that Michael Wornum knew precisely what was going on with us.

Our biggest problem, and one that would haunt us into the future, was a last shot at us by the BCDC staff in the form of a twenty-year time limit and review of the permit (as though there weren't already enforcement remedies built into all permits). Normally a time limit would kill a project. What possible incentive would someone have to loan money or spend money on a project that might have no value, or, indeed, might become a liability at the end of twenty years, or be forced to jump through the same hoops all over again in order to be able to continue in operation? A gamble at best. We agreed to it at the last minute, though, because we didn't have the votes to override it—again, government shunning any responsibility (or credit) for our existence in the first place and because we were talking about an existing community that could be lost if we didn't agree. By that point, if it were my property, my instinct would have been to say phooey and let them go to war with us. I know Arques would have done so if he'd been present, and it wasn't an easy sell after the fact to get Arques to agree to the approved conditions. He could still have balked and that definitely would have ended the process. We took what we could get knowing there'd be a fight later, hopefully from a better position. It turned out it wasn't.

In contrast to the BCDC, the County of Marin, being closer to the residents of Marin, had listened to us and, I'd like to believe, were conscious of the county's shared responsibility for our problems, and made an effort to understand. Once they understood what we were trying to accomplish and why, they helped us proceed, consistent with their rules, instead of automatically taking an adversarial position as the BCDC staff had done.

The actions of the BCDC and the County of Marin—opposite sides of our coin—and my experience in dealing with government at all levels, indicates to me that politics carries far more weight than law in our society. While resorting to law and the courts is always an option to assert one's rights, the cost and the amount of time required to do so generally makes it a poor option, and thus, the favored solution is to go along with what government wants and just plan for high-end uses, which will justify the increased costs, or the wink and the nod. Almost everything to do with Waldo Point, in my experience, has been political and has been determined by which way the wind blew. A very expensive crapshoot indeed for someone trying to accomplish something on their property, particularly if there is a dispute, since the system favors those who get there first, who've already built, who's interests are already vested, and who are already connected and already contribute to election campaigns. And, lest we forget, all costs associated with the whole process are necessarily passed on to the end user, the consumer, you and me.

* * *

There were a number of items I couldn't back down on, control of those portions of the streets where our docks crossed being the last problem, and that had to be resolved at the county level.

By then, the number of new people living on the Arques property and the intersecting county streets without permission from anyone had grown, and many, in line with the times, were or had become militantly "anti-establishment." If you didn't agree with their philosophy, you were the enemy, except when it came to providing access, parking, garbage pickup, utilities, and of course, paying the taxes that subsidized their food stamps and welfare checks. Then we were just suckers. It was easy to get steamed when we let ourselves think about it. Our rent money not only paid for the people who were crashing on the property, but the government used our tax money to provide welfare checks and food stamps for many of them, as well as free attorneys later when they got busted for obstructing our dock work. It was not hard to conclude that they would have been less of a problem to everyone if so many of them hadn't been subsidized by the government (taxpayers), but instead had to work for their living (rather than having time on their hands to blame us for their problems, or for how they felt about the world, and to cook up schemes to get even).

One of my favorite cartoons from that period shows a young, well-dressed "hippie" couple discussing their plans for the day. He says to her, "I gotta split and pick up the ole unemployment check, then make it to the University to see what's holding up the Federal Education Grant, and then pick up the food stamps. You make it to the free clinic for your check-up, and pick up my new glasses at the health center, then go to the welfare department, and try to get an increase. I'll meet you later at the federal building for the demonstration against the stinkin' establishment." There must be comfort in feeling that you are a victim, that you are "one of the oppressed." You not only get to feel sorry for yourself, but it frees you from any personal responsibility and gives you an excuse to blame someone or something else for the things that you feel aren't going right in your life.

Had the new docks been built without the property owner having control of the streets where the docks crossed and without being able to use those parts of the streets for houseboat berths, the people who were opposed to everything would have felt compelled to move their boats to those locations, hang out on those sections of the docks, and would have performed their usual "in your face" behavior that was one of their trademarks. The paying tenants would have been denied the quiet enjoyment of the berths they were leasing, would eventually have withheld rent, the property owner would have had a continuing battle on his hands, and everything would have stayed nasty.

The movie *Helter Skelter* is an uncanny reminder to me of those years at Waldo Point. To my knowledge, we didn't have a psycho mass murderer in residence, but the mindless, often heartfelt I'm sure, eagerness of many to join up and be part of something, to be led, to not listen to contrary points of view, and to have someone or something to hate was certainly present, as well as a seeming propensity for self-destruction. Of course our gang at Waldo were generally more independent, smarter and more capable than the young people portrayed in the movie. Living on the water requires that.

My mother once told my sister and I that when she was a very young girl and her parents didn't let her or her brothers have or do something they wanted, which made them mad, they would say, "We are going to eat worms and you'll be sorry!" I always felt there was an element of that kind of thinking in our scene in those days.

I told the county, "No streets. No project." You can see empty spaces on East and West Piers in the Kappas lagoon where streets still belong to the county. Kappas didn't feel a need to control those streets, partly because Helen Kappas never lost control of her father's property, and partly because no one from our side of the levee seemed interested in being on their side.

One thing that has to be understood in all of this, if anything "wonderful" is to come of it, is that the people living on county streets, which included a majority of the militants, were tenants-at-will of the county, not tenants of Arques's. The county had already acknowledged the fact that the debris on their streets was their responsibility, but never once spoke up to take responsibility for all the people and boats and docks and utilities and cars and campers and buses and structures on their streets. It was always Arques's "fault" and his problem, and nobody on either side suggested otherwise. Us for tactical reasons and the county, I suppose, because then they would have had to do something about it instead of leaving the problem in our hands, which is where I wanted it, and apparently where the county wanted it too. In that regard, whether a deliberate decision or not, we owe the county a debt of gratitude because our survival as a community depended on us solving the "houseboat problem."

To handle the street issue, I suggested to Deputy County Counsel Joe Forest that Arques buy the streets where they crossed his planned docks, without having any idea of whether or not Arques would go for it. Mr. Forest told us that the county didn't have the right to sell the streets under public trust law, but that they could lease them, which is what we did in a quid pro quo exchange of fifty-year leases (Arques's outboard property for sections of inboard streets).

Finally we were at a point where we could apply for the actual building permits for the entire project. We'd gotten our pilot and master plans through the county and BCDC, received okays from, among others, the US Army Corps of Engineers, the Sausalito-Marin City Sanitary District, the Marin Municipal Water District, PG&E, Parks and Recreation, Fish and Game, the US Department of the Interior, the State of California Water Resources Control Board, and I had hand-carried our fire plan to Woodacre for the Marin County Fire Marshall's signature. Over time we'd also separately satisfied others who'd offered objections in response to various application notices. An organization that had objected during one of our first hearings in Marin, but was voted down, was the Marin Conservationists. Being local, it surprised me that they hadn't done us the courtesy of at least talking to either Hugh Lawrence or myself before taking a position on our application. We were told at the time not to worry about them, "They oppose everything."

Many years later at Michael Wornum's death party—he was dying of cancer and wanted to say goodbye with a party—I'd had a few and was talking to Margaret Azevedo who at the time was on the California Coastal Commission. Something about past political battles came up, and I made the comment, an obvious exaggeration, that in my experience a conservationist in Marin was someone who lived in a redwood house and was opposed to logging—"I got mine, fuck you." Margaret looked at me with that trademark sparkle in her eyes, cocked her head, and said, "You know, you're right." Margaret Azevedo was a champion conservationist, but she never lost sight of other individual's needs or rights. Strange bedfellows, dopers, and conservationists trying to stop us, for entirely different reasons, I'm sure.

In all, during the planning process, I counted forty boards, commissions, agencies, groups, and individuals who sat in judgment with absolute or partial veto power over the survival of houseboat berthing on the Richardson Bay houseboat properties in county waters. You could probably double that number today.

* * *

Five years, seven months, and fourteen days after we entered the planning process, I picked up our actual building permits for the approved plan for the entire property. It would be another year and eight months before Donlan J. Arques leased his property with an option to buy, complete with the street lease and building permits, to Lewis E. Cook Jr., who would bring with him the capital to start serious work under the permits and the guts to stick with it through extraordinary times and despite extraordinary government actions and inaction.

Arques had told me he would not use his permits himself because he refused to encumber his property with bank loans, which would put him at the mercy of both the lenders and the government. He'd also once told me that he would only do the project himself if he could take his time and do it mostly out of income. That might have worked if everyone who benefited from the use of his property had paid berthage and if government relaxed all the announced time limits— time limits that proved to be fantasies in any case—for starting and completing the improvements.

I believed that if circumstances had been different and everyone had backed Arques by paying their berthage from the outset, and I'd been able to hand him a check each month after paying all expenses, he would have seen the benefit of sticking with the houseboats. He could easily have pulled funds out of other assets to accelerate dock construction and would have been justified by a higher return on his money, something he took seriously, just as we all do. We could have avoided the houseboat war, huge expenses, and forty-two years in a bullpie "planning process".

Originally, Arques had just thought of the houseboats as a way to pay his property taxes while he waited for property values to rise and the opportune moment to sell out, as he had done with the Johnson Street yard. Getting plan approvals and permits for the entire property, as a houseboat harbor, changed all that and fixed the use and the value. Then it was just a question of whether he would build it himself or sell to someone who would. He opted to sell.

Hugh Lawrence negotiated the property lease on Arques's behalf with Lew Cook's attorneys, while I did what I could to keep the project and the permits alive. To that end, during the lease negotiations, Lew loaned Arques one hundred thousand dollars on a first deed of trust which I used mostly to pay old property taxes, old bills, buy some materials, and pay for some labor. I also paid myself ten thousand dollars at Arques's suggestion. That was my big payday.

From the beginning, money from Arques was not a consideration. I supported myself with my marine work. What I did at Waldo Point was more along the lines of having a tiger by the tail and not being willing to turn loose for fear of hurting everyone in sight, including myself. I also felt an obligation to Arques because he had let me buy used equipment on credit that made it possible for me to start my small business.

All in all, it was an extraordinary experience I couldn't have bought with money, and I was certainly never bored, nor did I ever feel there was something else I should be doing. I think A.E. Housman was on to something when he wrote:

> Could man be drunk for ever
> With liquor, love, or fights.
> Lief should I rouse of mornings,
> And Lief lie down of nights.

> But men at whiles are sober,
> And think by fits and starts,
> And if they think they fasten
> Their hands upon their hearts.[i]

I met Lew Cook for the first time just before he took over and outlined the policies I had been operating by and the special deals I had in place for several of the older or infirm tenants. Lew said he would honor my commitments, and he did. Lew Cook is one of the most honorable men I have met—and that, under the pressure of very trying circumstances.

Chapter 10

It Starts

Lew Cook formally took over on January 1, 1977 and I sent an announcement letter to that effect to all tenants. Almost immediately, Piro Caro, an old radical from the 1930s who for years had occupied the entire upper deck of the ferryboat *San Rafael*—his rent was forty dollars per month, one of the special deals for an older resident—organized and called for a general meeting on the *Charles Van Damm*. He told a mostly receptive audience of young people, dopers, free spirits, revolutionaries looking for a cause, drop-ins, and ordinary dead beats that they were all going to be thrown out by evil developers and that they should lay down in front of the bulldozers. During the years I'd known him, Piro had always been against codes and government regulations, and had even tried, after the property was already leased to Cook, to get Arques to lease it to him instead, but he had never once said anything to me or, to my knowledge to Arques, directly opposing the efforts to make houseboats legal. He was familiar with both my policies and what was at stake for both Arques and the houseboat owners.

It should be noted here that even those who supported the plan would rather have had the county go away and leave things as they were before the flood of dopers and crashers. Of course it would be nice to have adequate utilities and better water pressure, and a sewer to hook up to, and less mud puddles during the winter. We also understood the necessity of giving Arques an economic incentive to continue with houseboats as the main use on his property, instead of a yacht harbor and/or a hotel for instance.

Piro was "the peoples'" elder statesman and an impressive and convincing speaker. The young ladies in particular loved to sit at his knee and listen. He also had a young, red-haired beauty for a mistress. We youngsters were jealous. But, this was to be his last hurrah, and "so what" if someone got hurt by believing what he told them. I also don't think he ever expressed gratitude to Arques, whose permits he was trying to scuttle, for the years of very cheap housing he'd enjoyed on Arques's property, or for the fact that he was assured a lifetime place to live where he was, just like several of the older or infirm who couldn't pay more than they already were. I guess he felt he was special, and it was his due.

At the same time Piro was busy raising the rabble, Arques, when questioned about the change-over by some of the same people Piro was appealing to, told them that they were all going to be frozen out, essentially repeating what Piro was saying and encouraging them to fight the project (which he had just leased to Lew Cook). Had he told them the truth, that the free-loading days were over, but that they would have a legal place for their boats, the revolt would probably have fizzled or at least not have had the support of many key figures who both knew and were in one way or another indebted to Arques.

If any one person had the standing and moral authority to prevent or stop the fight, despite the influence of outsiders, it was Arques. I went to see him and asked that he make a statement to that effect and he turned me down flat. I think he saw the protesters as a last means of expressing his anger at being forced by government to do something against his will, which in effect made that small army of young people his surrogates (as he cried all the way to the bank). Except in one short letter to Piro asking cooperation, Arques never expressed concern for—nor do I think even considered how the things he was saying might effect his loyal—paying tenants who had made his valuable permits possible. What Arques committed to writing—possible evidence in a court action—and what he said in person (hearsay), were often quite different.

Reportedly, I suppose trying to look good to his listeners of the moment, he also said, at least once, that he had nothing to do with the permits, that it was all my doing. I'd been promoted to property owner without knowing it, and yet Arques kept the profit derived from the plan approvals and permits when he leased the property, so I guess I was just a temporary owner.

Hugh Lawrence was furious with Arques, his client, about things Arques was saying, knowing that Arques was giving Lew Cook grounds for a legal action and possible damages.

With the signing of the lease by Arques and Cook, Hugh Lawrence's involvement with Waldo Point Harbor ended, except as a tenant, but he continued to represent Arques until Arques's death in 1993. Hugh still lives on A-Dock with his lovely and accomplished wife Patricia, and along with his law practice, was for many years involved in matters related to maritime transport.

* * *

Piro's "bloody bulldozer" speech on the Van Damm was the official start of the houseboat war. It was characterized in most of the media as "The People vs. The Developers," which were the best buzzwords to inspire outsiders to join the fight and keep the fight and the story alive. In short order, our detractors became experts at feeding the press, being sure to give advance notice, particularly to TV stations, of scheduled demonstrations. The demonstrators would periodically check with the harbor office to get our work schedule, so they would know when to demonstrate and when to call the media.

There were few secrets on the waterfront. We, of course, took it for granted that there would be a demonstration whenever we did anything.

The majority of the media obviously appreciated the help from the newsworthy demonstrators as it made their job of reporting much easier. No research was required. There were exceptions, the most notable being Doris Berdahl who wrote for the *Marin Scope*, a Sausalito weekly newspaper. From early in the planning process, Doris had spent the time necessary to talk to all sides, got to know the issues as well as the individuals involved, and wrote well-considered and thoughtful articles. Having covered Sausalito politics (we are in the county, not Sausalito) she was familiar with how the law and government worked.

Margaret Azevedo, who wrote a column for the *Marin Independent Journal*, had a lot to say later on. Having long worked inside government and having participated in the decision-making process under which we received our plan approvals, Margaret knew the system, the law, and people. She wrote on August 5, 1978 about the "moral amnesia that seems to affect members of the protestors' group, the knack for omitting essentials," of "the curious mental construct employed to obscure the real nature of their acts, perhaps from the perpetrators themselves," of the "highly developed sense of their own virtue," and "huge oversimplification(s)" regarding what they saw as "the sordid demands of property against the rights of human beings to live as they choose." She quoted Joseph Cropsey, political scientist at the University of Chicago, who argued in an essay on conservatism and liberalism that "The constitutional protection of property is an essential civil instrument by which the fragile natural right to life and liberty are safeguarded. . . Each human being constitutes a petty Monarchy within the borders of the political community. Unequipped, he is naked. With his adjunct property his monarchy is a defensible sanctuary." (I guess that made me a defensible sanctuariest.) She said a lot more in the same piece which gave a sense of the time and place.

Dick Spotswood, a columnist for the *Marin Independent Journal* (but a Mill Valley counsel member at the time), in discussing one protestor's proposal to move twenty of their houseboats next to a bayside park in Mill Valley, is quoted in an August 18, 1981 *Independent Journal* article as saying, "I certainly do not want to see a houseboat community established in Mill Valley. It would be disastrous. I regard some of the people in the houseboat community as freeloaders. They don't pay property taxes generally. A good many of them have made a mess of the Gate 5 area. It's the '60s generation gone to seed."

It seemed that most reporters, though, perhaps under pressure from deadlines, just went to the tombs for their background, and then added the barebones of whatever was currently happening, including names and quotes. They usually missed the heart of the matter and their stories could easily be read by the protestors as tacitly dignifying or as outright encouragement of their position (and their tactics).

Not long ago I was trading stories with an old friend who was one of the more active participants in the opposition. He told me that some of the guys who came over from Berkeley believed this was going to be the start of the American Revolution. "They were scary," he said. My friend was always a gentleman in personal contacts, no matter what else was taking place, except when he was high on meth, then he was paranoid and surly. Once he positioned his skiff under the leads of my pile driver and put his arms around the pile I was about to drive, so I knelt down close to him and quietly told him not to hold tight because he might get splinters or burns from the creosote. He thanked me, I lowered and drove the pile, and he didn't get splinters or creosote burns. He had gotten deeply involved in the drug scene, and that's probably what put him on the other side. He presently owns and lives in a large, valuable houseboat across the dock from where I drove that pile.

Many of the protestors who actually lived on the property got so carried away with the rhetoric and the actions of the moment, that they forgot we might all have to live together when the dust settled.

* * *

In August of 1977, there were at least two explosions at a Sausalito PG&E substation. After the second explosion, one of our resident security guards, Bob Poppit, got a call at home in the middle of the night saying, in reference to the explosions, "This is a warning," and then the caller hung up. Bob was living with his wife and baby daughter on their small houseboat at the time. I have notes that unexploded bombs were found in the Pacific-Union Building and the Olympic Club in San Francisco. I believe Lew Cook had connections with both of those organizations at the time.

August of 1977 was a busy month. Not only were bombs set off at the Sausalito PG&E substation, and the threat that we were next, but the protestors' lead attorney told Doug Maloney, Marin's chief counsel, that he'd heard there were snipers gearing up and that the parking area we were working on (that now serves D or Liberty Dock) had also been mined. Figuring it was just another attempt to slow the work, Ted Rose and I took turns running a small tractor back and forth over the entire area early the next day before the contractor's crew arrived. We didn't blow up and nobody was shot. So much for psychological warfare.

Over time, their lead attorney and others announced scheduled demonstrations on at least one radio station, encouraging others to join the action. Protesters were recruited from around the Bay Area and came by land and water, including on one occasion a group of elderly Filipinos bussed over from the International Hotel fight in San Francisco. I happened to be on Gate 5 Road when they arrived, was first to reach them, and was able to convince them that they were being "used" by one side in what was essentially an internal dispute between residents. They remained on the bus and left. Thank God. If some of those fragile men and women had been pushed to the front in a scuffle, they could have been seriously hurt which would have served to escalate the violence. Putting mothers and babies in the front line was a favorite tactic.

Over time, numerous political figures, from the mayor of Sausalito to the governor of California, were solicited by the protestors to gain support for their positions. Friends usually alerted me to such requests, and so I sent short letters to the indicated individuals advising them that there were two sides to the issue within the community and asking that they inform themselves before taking a position. Nobody responded to my letters, so I don't know if they had any effect, or if the recipients were just being smart and avoiding involvement in a local political controversy. Only a few minor characters answered the call and then not for very long.

The protestors were not successful in widening the conflict, which was a major objective. After the December 12ᵗʰ riot, one of the protestors was quoted in a Sunday, December 18, 1977 *San Francisco Examiner/Chronicle* article as saying, "People were pushed to fight to protect their homes. . . It's going to reach a point where someone will get killed. We'll have another Kent State and a whole outraged nation." Fear of that prospect was obviously a factor in government's reluctance to enforce the law evenly across the board. Acts that would put you or me (acting alone) in hot water were often ignored when perpetrated by a member of a group protest.

While the protestors' outside leadership, at least, were hoping for something like a Kent State and geared their physical tactics accordingly, the rest of us, i.e., the property owner, the tenants, the county, and even the BCDC, were trying to achieve the more mundane objective of accommodating some of the plan additions and code changes the protestors had originally requested.

One of the professional "community organizers" attracted to our little war was particularly accomplished in media, legal, and protest tactics. Until near the end, that is, when our locals became tired of taking orders from him and he left, perhaps for more important battles. The protestors' numbers in terms of watercraft (and certainly people) dramatically increased during the violent period that lasted <u>more than four years</u>.

* * *

Early in the affair some members of the opposition, mostly women, had come to my office, which was by then on the *Eight Brothers*—the 8' x 8' office I'd used for years wasn't big enough any longer—and we had a number of long, friendly discussions. I had a feeling that the friendliness was staged, and the talks didn't really go anywhere. The discussions were mostly a repeat of what we'd already gone over: That we, the rest of the community, and management would support their newly expressed wish to keep their group of thirty-five boats together where they were already located (outboard of the *Charles Van Damm*), instead of only offering them berths on the five approved docks, and that the new property owner was willing to go back into the planning process for that purpose. One of their numbers, Pete Retondo, had prepared a very professional plan showing a proposed layout for their thirty-five boats, and we used that as a basis for the discussions.

We then arranged a more inclusive meeting to pursue that end at a Gate 5 restaurant, in the same building where I'd first seen Juanita in action years before. Present were representatives of the county planning department, the BCDC, the protestors, other residents, and the property owner, and all parties agreed in principal to the requested plan change and some related changes to the code. We left that meeting feeling something had been accomplished. We were mistaken. What had been gained by the discussions in my office and at the Gate 5 restaurant with government officials, and the follow up talks with planners regarding code changes was time for the protestors to prepare and file a massive lawsuit and get a temporary restraining order to stop construction. As Stalin is quoted as saying, "Agreements are like pie crusts—made to be broken."

The next step was an eight-day preliminary injunction hearing in Marin County Superior Court to determine whether the restraining order should be made permanent pending final disposition of the underlying lawsuit, which could take years. The plaintiff's attorneys subpoenaed everything to do with Lew Cook's business and his limited partners and called them all to testify. If their hope was to show fire and aggression by heartless businessmen, that fell flat. The investors were just people with money who invested conservatively and who had been offered about what they could have earned in a well-managed mutual fund. They had no hand in the business. It was also hard to make the case that it was evil to invest in a business that used Arques's permits to give houseboats a future by making them legal. On our side, the county, which had a serious interest in seeing the project go forward, called their building inspector, Mr. Larson, the county fire marshal, and others, who paraded pictures, maps, and testimony about how awful things were at Waldo Point and how it was urgent to fix up the place for health and safety reasons. The county fire marshal said they should put a fence around us.

I was called to testify and spent a lot of time in the witness box explaining and justifying my policies and detailing the work we'd done so far under the permits. There was a lot of sarcasm in the questions by the protestor's lead attorney, which inspired me to respond in an unkind manner, and I was rather quickly made a hostile witness (which was accurate). In the end, he probably won on posturing and innuendo, but I won on the facts because I knew what I was talking about and he didn't—he'd gotten most of his information from his clients. Their only serious challenge was to the continuing validity of our permits, asserting no work had been done within the required time limit to start work. We beat them on that primarily because I'd kept a handwritten daily log in the normal course of business, something Arques had suggested years before. I hadn't been able to do much work, mostly paid for out of rents, and mostly demolition, but work had been performed, money had been spent, and the permits vested.

I never understood the logic of the protestors' attack on our permits. If they'd won—if they'd been able to show the permits had lapsed—that probably would have been the end of houseboats on the Arques property. Lew Cook might well have backed out at that point since the value of the property was in the permits, and Arques certainly would never have gone back into the planning process if the property reverted to him. The paying tenants would have stopped paying rent, a series of abatement actions would inevitably have followed, with no basis to negotiate, and the property would eventually have been cleared and then resold for a different use.

Maybe the protestors thought they could scare everyone into abandoning the property to them so they would be left alone to do as they pleased: to be their own landlord, to collect money from each other (and from us) in order to pay the utilities, etc., and to make rules for each other, (and for us) about who and where they and we could tie-up, and perhaps in turn, would have suffered an internal revolt.

Successful revolutionaries do tend to become the systems they say they hate, often worse, and if the old protestors' "rights" had been challenged by new protestors, would they have gone to the legal system to protect their "rights" or just gone to war and been satisfied to let the matter be determined by whoever had the biggest gun?

The preliminary injunction hearing was their first and most serious challenge to what we were trying to accomplish, and it was denied. From then on it was a long series of demonstrations, sabotage, arson, break-ins, and lawsuits directed at the harbor, and multiple acts of vandalism and violence and threats directed against the residents, including women and children, who supported the harbor, and also against those who worked for the harbor. Few of those acts rose to the level to being "newsworthy" because they were usually perpetrated at night, were not announced to the press, nor were they performed in the presence of the press. The press were normally here only when invited for the formally planned demonstrations, and any violence at those events was usually directed only at sheriff deputies, which was apparently considered normal, and made good copy. (I don't suggest that all protestors were bloody-minded or countenanced such behavior, nor did they stop it.) Numerous times we suggested to members of the press and to politicians that they spend time with us, particularly at night and unannounced, so they could get a feel for what we were experiencing. Nobody accepted our invitations.

For long periods of time, more money was being spent by the harbor on security and attorney's fees than on construction. I have one old summary of security-related incidents that were reported to my office by tenants and employees during a three-month period starting in November 1980. The list includes ten incidents of verbal harassment, including one directed at a visitor with a young child in a rowboat, a death threat against a security guard, a promise to poison plants in the new landscaping, a slow drive-by with shouted obscenities, six rock throwing incidents that resulted in broken windows in a houseboat and a rear window broken in a moving vehicle, a visiting couple refusing to return to the harbor in fear for their baby's life, ten tires slashed, thefts (including fire hoses cut and nozzles stolen), a car broken into and items taken, a car stolen and found by police in Mill Valley, a workboat and engine stolen, several incidents of gas siphoned from tenants' cars, a battery stolen, one hundred fifty feet of heavy electrical cable cut and taken, seven shots fired (three through car windows and one that just missed a tenant and hit a houseboat), a county road sign rammed by a car, protestors' children being told that harbor and B-Dock people wanted to kill them and then encouraged to throw rocks and use a sling-shot (a couple of the children told us this because they didn't believe their adults), numerous parking stickers either scratched up or peeled off of residents cars, more fire hoses cut, graffiti death threats referring to the blood of our children being smeared all over A-, B-, C-, and D-Docks (they missed E-Dock) in large letters in the women's restroom in the Trieste Cafe in downtown Sausalito, lumber thrown at a security guard in the South 40 (E-Dock) at 0430 one morning, wires cut to two lights in the B-Dock parking lot, paint thinner thrown on a tenant in the South 40 (". . . didn't want anyone except artists like themselves. . . "), an attempted houseboat break-in, and if all that wasn't sufficient, six dogs were poisoned with hamburger containing ground glass and rat poison. One dog died, the others just suffered.

Those tenant- and employee-related incidents reported to my office during that three-month period were about on par with the entire four plus years of protests. The sheriff was called in some of those cases, and I'm sure many things I was unaware of occurred, possibly reported only to the sheriff or not reported to anyone, such as the everyday, run-of-the-mill death threats. Organized demonstrations and related activities were more intense.

It is informative to note how laws are actually enforced. In our case, for instance, the threats, and acts of violence employed by organized protestors were treated by government as legitimate negotiating tools. At some point unlawful actions had been transformed into expressions of free speech, providing there was enough people perpetrating the illegal acts—certainly not an unusual phenomena if we are to believe the following article in the June 5, 1978 *Fortune* magazine:

Peace Returns to Stoughton Wisconsin
Stoughton, Wisconsin, April 21. Pursuant to stipulation, the Board ordered the union to cease engaging in mass picketing, hampering and/or blocking the ingress and egress of vehicles or persons; throwing rocks, stones, eggs, and tomatoes at, and breaking win-

dows of buildings; threatening damage to vehicles; throwing rocks, stones, eggs, and tomatoes at vehicles; slashing tires, severing air lines, cutting electric wires, and smashing headlights of vehicles; throwing soda or a like substance onto vehicles; smashing the windshields of vehicles; breaking off, bending or otherwise damaging the antennas and outside mirrors of vehicles; and spraying or splattering paint on vehicles.

The union was further ordered to cease placing spiked boards beneath the wheels of vehicles; jabbing picket sign standards into the grills of vehicles; threatening employees with physical harm, with unspecified harm, and with picket signs and two by fours; hitting and jabbing employees with picket signs; hitting with fists, kicking, shoving, and spitting on employees; following vehicles driven by employees, forcing the vehicles off the road and beating the drivers; threatening employees with harm to their spouses; engaging in surveillance of employees; and in any like or related manner, restraining or coercing employees of Stoughton Trailers, Inc.[ii]

Government's willingness to talk and negotiate while other citizens are being subjected to threats and violence legitimizes and prolongs the successful use of such tactics. Professional "community organizers" not only recognize and rely on the political considerations that motivate such a non-response by government to such activity, but they also know that it puts them in a position to extort not just concessions but also money. Money, and the power that goes with it, is the real prize for conducting such illegal activity, and that is exactly what occurred in our case. Such payoffs have the side effect of promoting dependence on, and in turn, enhancing the authority of the "state"—which the rest of us are taxed to pay for—instead of citizens being expected and required to be responsible for their actions and to exercise initiative and personal effort to advance their interests, which instead of creating dependence, promotes independence and protects our liberties.

I wonder how long our little houseboat war would have lasted if government had flatly and publicly refused to talk while the protestors employed threats and violence and had enforced the law equally while they were at it? Since our property owner had already said he was willing to make the originally requested changes in the plan, and government had agreed to those changes in principal, the end result, except for free money, would have been the same for the boat owners who were protesting. George Eliot put the whole thing very nicely in her book *Middlemarch* when she wrote, "Don't you think men overrate the necessity for humoring everybody's nonsense, till they get despised by the very fools they humor?"

I'm sure that if the same mob methods had been employed in the communities of Mill Valley or Tiburon or Belvedere, such antics would have been cracked down on immediately, because the politicians in those towns would have been voted out of office (been out on their butts) in the next elections if they hadn't insisted that the law be enforced equally to protect all their residents' rights. Much as I prefer a distant government, it was too distant for us at that time, and the law-abiding residents of our community didn't have the numbers necessary, or display the militant behavior required, to earn the influence we needed with the county. Which, in an entitlement culture, is one of the problems with being collectable. Unlike "the people" you have to pay your own attorney's fees if you step outside the law. The result was we had to do the heavy lifting ourselves in the absence of equal law enforcement. The protestors clearly had an advantage.

* * *

I suspect that most of us at one time or another have agonized over how our society, our legislatures, and our bureaucracies impose their will (and the associated paperwork) on us in various aspects of our everyday lives. Some rules make sense, like driving on only one side of the street and having panic bars on restaurant and theater exits. Other rules are unnecessarily intrusive or restrictive, needlessly expensive or even harmful, and cry out to be changed or dropped entirely. Many rules are associated with a promise of cradle to grave security, which experience has shown tends to emasculate us in mind and body. Kind of like modern cars with all their bells and whistles that relieve us from thinking and do everything for us but drive themselves, until they get an electrical or computer glitch, then into the shop for someone else to fix. We are being "saved" from the hard choices we need to experience in life, if we are to retain the thinking skills necessary to own our own lives. To paraphrase Captain Kirk, we need challenges in order to thrive.

At our country's founding, we were blessed with the challenge of unlimited space and opportunities in a "new world." We were freed from rigid old-world class, church, and government control and eventually spurred to create our marvelous Constitution, which has made us the freest and most prosperous nation in human history.

Yet now, instead of expecting and encouraging individuals to work hard, develop self-reliance, and enjoy the freedoms associated with thinking, active, responsible citizens, we have a self-serving political culture of big brother that penalizes initiative—both when we are alive and after we're dead—and in the end would take over and relieve us of all responsibility, and with it, our freedom. It is in the best interest of those in power to acquire authority over the rest of us in as many areas of our lives as possible, and to make us dependent on them. That is not in our best interest.

In the end, though, we generally abide by the rules we are handed; we want to believe they represent the intelligence and will of our free society as delivered by our elected representatives and also because we respect that our Constitution provides constructive ways to change laws we don't like. We believe in majority rule anchored in a foundation of individual rights, including the right to be secure in our property, the recognition and protection of it, whether a hammer, a house, or the money in our pockets—being the foundation upon which all civil liberties rest and without which individual freedom cannot exist. That is the deal we made with each other a long time ago as the best way to conduct human affairs without constant warfare, and we know that it's the best system that has ever been devised by and between human beings.

I believe that in our heart of hearts, all of us want the freedom to live our lives as we choose, and we wish or yearn for honest representation and a just order in our universe so we can get on with our lives without constantly watching our backs. This, of course, puts a great burden of expected wisdom on our elected leaders, and they are often <u>not</u> up to the task. Or they may cynically pander to whomever and whatever they think can get them the most votes in order to get and keep themselves in power, which of course is the whole point, good and bad, of being in politics. Alas, they are human like the rest of us. Political power does not always attract the best people, and when it does, it often seduces them once they get it, and they forget the responsibility that goes with power, if they ever understood it in the first place.

At Waldo Point most of us tried to abide by the rules. Others who lived next door to us on the same kinds of floatation, drank the same beer, drove the same cars, had attended the same schools, and enjoyed the same opportunities available to all free men were excused from following the rules and instead were rewarded for violent behavior. What's wrong with that picture?

I would add here that just having opportunities is never enough to be "successful" in anything. Succeeding in life requires actually cracking a book to find out how things work, asking questions, paying attention, and finally some old fashioned self-discipline and hard work, what used to be the common ethic in America. It's true that the rich get richer and the poor stay poor, but as Ric Edelman says, "It's because the rich continue to do what made them rich and the poor continue to do what makes them poor." Chance or luck can have an affect on life, but it's mostly the choices each of us make each day that determine where we are.

To say that many of us at Waldo Point lost faith in our elected leaders and their spawned bureaucracies is an understatement. Who are these men and women who are so powerful and arrogant they can decide which citizens must obey the law and which citizens get a pass and, on top of that, have the gall to use our money to reward the violence that was directed against us? I don't believe for a moment that the illegal drug business, for one, could survive at its present level alongside an honest, responsible adult government peopled by true public servants. There should be a pill for enlarged egos.

* * *

When it was time to build the docks, I wanted to start in the South 40, a kind of hot spot, thinking that would shorten the war. I was overruled and we started with A-Dock at the north end of the property, an area that was occupied by "friendlies." A-Dock was built with minimal interference and immediately occupied, both for security reasons and to clear space for construction of B-Dock, which was later re-named *Issaquah* Dock after the nearby-grounded ferryboat, *Issaquah*.

The ferryboat *Issaquah* was reportedly built in 1913/14 on Lake Washington's east shore and spent it's early years mostly carrying people and cargo between Mercer Island, Issaquah, and Seattle Washington. In 1918, it was sold to the Rodeo-Vallejo Ferry System in the San Francisco Bay Area and worked the Carquinez Straits between Rodeo and Vallejo until the Carquinez Bridge opened. From 1929, it operated on various runs around the bay until it was taken out of service in 1948. Later, when *Issaquah* was moved to Waldo Point, it was intact, complete with boilers and engine, and at a compact one hundred fourteen feet, pretty as a picture according to Bud Fensler, who tried to buy it from Arques not long after it arrived. Arques refused to sell and instead had Lindsey Cage, who lived and operated a scrap yard on Arques's property in Marinship (and was *kind of a sage* to some of us), remove the machinery to sell as scrap, causing an immediate hog in the vessel. When I first saw it, worms had done the rest and only the main deck and superstructure were still intact and savable. I included the three existing ferryboats in our master plan: *Issaquah* and *Charles Van Damm*, which were close to each other at the north end of the property, and *San Rafael*, which was located in the South 40 and was in the same condition as *Issaquah*.

I had hoped to get Juanita back on the *Van Damm*, providing I could talk her into hiring a competent manager. She was perfect for our neighborhood. I also figured that a successful commercial use might relieve some of the pressure on the rest of us to provide Arques a return commensurate with the value of his property.

Except for *City of Seattle*, which was later put on a concrete barge, *Charles Van Damm* was possibly the last intact wooden ferryboat on the west coast. It was landlocked in its own stagnant saltwater pond, which protected it from worm damage, and it was definitely restorable to its original condition sans engine and machinery, for which ballast could have been substituted. As for *Issaquah* and *San Rafael*, we could have driven piles around them, jacked them up, and supported them on beams with additional bearing from their intact, mud-protected bottoms as was traditionally done with almost all arks at Waldo Point and those still remaining elsewhere in the Bay Area. They would have continued as residences topside with possibly some community serving uses on their weather decks.

* * *

Pile driving commenced with B-Dock and proceeded with little interference until we got to the east end of the straightaway section. We started work that morning facing a flotilla of anchored small boats crossing the T with the intent of blocking further progress. Their lead attorney was standing proudly in the bow of one of the boats determined to see that his client's rights were not abused and ready to take names and pictures of all offenders. However, they either hadn't studied our plans, which were public for all to see, or had miscalculated, because they were too far out. We just turned right and proceeded to drive piles for the short leg of the L in a southerly direction until the job was completed. The protestors, whose anchors were well set, and maybe because they were embarrassed by their mistake, didn't change position to try to block us and eventually left.

For security, we rigged a floating log boom all the way around B-Dock as we proceeded, driving temporary piles to hold it, and later we rigged lights underneath the dock and guarded it twenty-four hours a day.

My old dock had disappeared and part of the area it had occupied was filled and became the corner of Gate 6 Road. The harbor office, now on *Eight Brothers*, stayed relatively in the same position and was now near the entrance to the new B-Dock.

Following the pile driving, during the deck and utility phase of B-Dock construction, a section of dock close to shore and close to occupied boats was torched in the middle of the night, but I was able to put out the fire with buckets of salt water before the fire department arrived. A sixteen-foot section of deck, supporting stringers, and plumbing had to be replaced. It was the first arson fire, and that's when lights went underneath the docks, and we started round-the-clock security in construction sites and for the newly completed docks. Much later, after B-Dock was occupied and the log boom removed, the protestors chained one of the biggest houseboats to the high pressure gas main at high tide—again in the middle of the night—in hopes of causing a break when the tide dropped and possibly starting what could have been a major fire involving occupied houseboats. We lucked out. They had again miscalculated, and due to the angle of the chain to the boat, not enough weight was applied to do the job.

That large houseboat, now called *Dragon Boat*, had started as a 22' x 7' wood barge with a tiny house with only sitting headroom called *Psycholone*. The owner chose houseboat status long before we got our permits and paid full berthage until the property changed hands and then sold out for a healthy profit. If she had stayed, she'd probably have expanded the boat herself, as many of the smaller boat owners have done. When I originally asked her whether she wanted houseboat status with a future berth in the re-built harbor or to be considered a "small boat,"—a non-descriptive term I coined—and pay less berthage with the understanding she'd move off the property when we all had to come up to code (and that it might be expensive to bring a boat as small as hers up to that code), she thought about it awhile, and said, "Houseboat." She was a very smart young lady. At the time, most of us could only see the looming costs of bringing our boats up to code, what we accepted as a necessary evil if we wanted to stay. Few of us anticipated the great increase in value that would occur when we did become legal.

After rigging lights under B-Dock, we discovered that they attracted small fish, which in turn attracted bigger fish, and one of our resident volunteer guards, Robert Rainey, a Vietnam veteran known affectionately as Ducko, caught a large bass one night that rated a banquet and a party in the office. At the time, any excuse for a party was acceptable. We once had a birthday party for Ducko, who possessed a wicked sense of humor, so I prepared a large concrete cake for him complete with real icing and candles. It was a hard joke to follow.

When a state appellate court issued a stay of a December 27, 1977 Marin County Superior Court order barring obstruction of work in the harbor, Ducko expressed his views on the subject to Judge Elkington, who had been quoted in an *Examiner* article about the stay:

To: Judge Elkington of State Appellate Court.
Subject: H. Weinstein's *Examiner* article 1.17.78.
Dear sweet, kind, loving and thoughtfully considerate Judge Elkington,

I, as a paying tenant of Gate 5 Waldo Point, Sausalito, would like to personally thank you for your decision regarding a certain barge which was deliberately sunk here.

Your decision makes it perfectly clear that the best way for me to thank you would be for me to move onto your property, claiming said property as my own, illegally build a residence that is a fire, health, and safety hazard, illegally hook up to your utilities allowing you to pay the bills, block access to your home, damage your home by acts of vandalism, threaten you and all the members of your family—no matter sex or age—verbally and with firearms, and physically assault you with whatever comes to hand (boards, bricks, steel scrap, buckets of water, oars, chains).

In addition, I can party all night in the two hundred-decibel range and scream obscenities in the middle of the night, just when you think you are finally going to get a decent night's sleep.

Perchance I could pass the word that your driveway is mined and stack wrecked cars all over it, just prior to declaring your driveway a combination wild river, children's playground, organic garden, and national hysterical landmark!

If you, in response to these actions on my part, were to request assistance from any law enforcement agency, and they were to charge me with a crime, I would automatically be accorded "rights" that are not afforded a common citizen. I could then demand a civil rights commission inquisition on the grounds that the arresting officer did not say "Mother, may I" before handcuffing me without an umbrella on a rainy day.

Once again, thank you. I'm sure your decision would have been the same were you living here.

Dig it!!!

R.D. Rainey
Gate 5
Sausalito
cc. *Chronicle*
I.J.
Marin Scope
Pacific Sun
New York Times[iii]

Thump, rattle, bang, crash. "Uh oh, sounds like Ranney fell asleep in the shower again." One of the resident volunteers pulling security in the harbor office was Arthur Ranney Johnson who also used the initials K.G.B.—I don't know where that came from. I'd met him in Fred's at table nine, our favorite local eating place and hangout, when he started coming in after his second divorce. He'd been living in Bolinas with his lovely second wife, whom he'd met while living and working in Spain, but now Ranney had to move from his place in Bolinas. The foreign affairs journal he wrote for had closed its San Francisco office and told him he'd have to move to New York if he wanted to keep his job. He decided to stay in California, which meant he was without a job and a home when I first met him.

I'd queried some conclusions he'd drawn in one of his articles, so that connection plus getting to know him at Fred's cemented our friendship. Knowing his situation, I offered him the use of an unfinished, unused space on *Eight Brothers* until he got another job and found a better place to live. He accepted, and when the nastiness started at Waldo Point, he offered to help with security in the office.

Ranney was a dignified, gentlemanly, slim, six feet four inches tall, and all the ladies thought he was the cat's meow, though he didn't act the lady's man. His main joy was to sit reading in whatever coffee shop or restaurant supplied the most stimulating conversation. He could and did discuss anything one wanted to bring up (he was a self-taught economist) along the lines of history, politics, and personalities—worldwide—to current nation-state status and economics. He read continuously and had filing cabinets packed with information on every subject, literally from A to Z, and was on every political mailing list for magazines and newsletters from around the world, as well as regularly getting *The Wall Street Journal, The Economist,* and *The New York Times.* And, he was a knowledgeable railroad buff with an extensive collection of periodicals and annual reports dating from well before the twentieth century. Although he had the ability to make money on stocks, he was content to earn just enough to pay his way in coffee shops and the specialty markets he frequented in San Francisco, where he bought exotic cheeses, olives, wines and other hard to find goodies. Mostly, he read, he discussed, and he charmed the ladies, with whom he was very discrete.

Another of Ranney's traits was a wry sense of humor. In Fred's, sitting quietly in the corner near the pay phone at table nine, he would occasionally, when no one was looking, shoot a peanut or a dry pea or a spit wad (or similar missile) at a friend sitting at another table or at the counter (in the same way you'd shoot a marble when you were a kid) and hit them in the head or neck. He rarely missed. He had big hands and was a practiced expert in the art. It took the rest of us a while to catch on to what he was doing, and we were sitting at the same table! He looked so innocent. Later he told us that when he was a young man working in his father's office in Chicago, he'd once put a dish of ammonia in front of a fan on a hot summer day. It forced an evacuation of the office and cost him his job. His father, from long experience, knew precisely who the culprit was. Later Ranney worked for oil companies and others around the world, spending a lot of time in Spain and some in Venezuela. He spoke fluent Spanish. Both kinds.

On one occasion, some of the opposition at Waldo Point had a meeting with Sheriff Howenstein (he never met with us) on a large houseboat temporarily berthed near the stern of *Eight Brothers*. In the dark, Ranney rigged two of his biggest speakers in the partially open back wall of *Eight Brothers* and then put on a record of a steam engine starting up and getting under way. *Hiss-chug, hiss-chug, faster and faster, louder and louder till you'd swear that a train was rushing directly at you.* Everyone came barreling out onto the back deck of the boat where the meeting was taking place to see what was happening, as Ranney and I held our sides in the dark, laughing. As the train sounds faded into the distance the meeting broke up and Sheriff Howenstein left.

Another time, Ranney got into a letter-to-the-editor debate in our Sausalito paper, the *Marin Scope*, with a local who'd fought in the Lincoln Brigade during the Spanish Civil War, in which we got a glimpse of Ranney's remarkable knowledge of that conflict and the contributing agendas of other countries and leaders.

Ranney hated to sleep, feeling it was a waste of time. Occasionally he'd pull security late at night and when relieved, he'd go to his apartment across the breezeway from the office for breakfast and to get cleaned up and then fall asleep in the shower. It happened at least twice while I was there. One of us would then go pound on his door to make sure he was all right, and shortly after he would appear, heading out to go shopping or to his favorite hangout (instead of to bed).

Now mostly in a wheelchair, he still reads constantly and still pulls the occasional practical joke on the staff or other residents in the nursing home where he lives.

* * *

Something we noticed besides fish while guarding B-Dock late at night was a small boat or boats running north at high speed without running lights in the natural channel just our side of the Strawberry Peninsula. With a little checking we found they were landing at the old railroad trestle where the line crosses the outflow from Tam Valley, southeast of Tam Junction. Guessing the next step, which experience told us involved drugs and probably the old Fireside Motel units behind El Roboso Mexican restaurant, another favorite eatery of ours, I took photos of boats, people, and places along with dates and vessel registration (or CF) numbers to the Drug Enforcement Administration (DEA) office in San Francisco. Their first question to me was, "Does this have anything to do with the houseboat war?" After I explained the circumstances of our discovery and that the information was not directly related to the houseboats, they finally agreed to accept the information I offered, saying, "Well, you've got the time, place, and the actors." They'd obviously gotten the hands-off directive about our little war. The nighttime boats continued their routine, but we got too busy to keep track of them or to follow up with the DEA.

The harbor office on *Eight Brothers* was manned twenty-four hours a day for over four years by harbor staff during work days and by resident volunteers during off-hours and weekends and holidays. Nothing was ever stolen from us during that period nor did we suffer any sabotage. The value of our people knowing their people was the best kind of security. Knowing your opposition and thus being able to forestall their activities in our kind of situation is the least destructive for both sides.

One of the residents who occasionally helped with security on *Eight Brothers* had graduated in New York with a degree in social services. She told us that her first job after college was to walk certain assigned streets in New York City handing out pamphlets with instructions on how to get welfare payments. Her boss made it clear that he wanted as many people signed up as possible so he could earn a promotion and a pay raise. Later she had occasion to observe some of her new clients collecting their welfare checks at a local post office and then signing them over to drug dealers who waited outside. Feeling that subsidizing the illegal drug business was an inappropriate use of taxpayers' money, she quit her secure job in the welfare department, gave up her hard-to-get apartment, and came to California. Much later, she went back to school and became a certified public accountant (CPA). Another sharp, independent lady.

During that same four-year-plus period, among other things, Lew Cook's office in San Francisco was broken into and documents stolen, at least five other fires were started including a serious one in the construction yard next to Bridgeway, a harbor attorney's office in Tiburon was firebombed, contractors equipment was sabotaged, and some of Lew Cook's investors were harassed at their homes.

Chapter 11

December 12, 1977

On December 12, 1977, after earlier aborted attempts had earned us an injunction against the protestors, we were scheduled to start work on D-Dock, now called Liberty Dock, and big resistance was promised and had been prepared. We staged at B-Dock, where we kept our floating equipment near the office. Sheriff deputies were stationed on long floats tied alongside my little pile driver, other deputies were loaded in small motorboats to accompany us and a Coast Guard boat stood by, well outboard of the property, the only time I recall them being present during our long conflict.

Usually, at that time, I worked with only one man, Ted Eitelbuss, also a houseboat owner. He took a lot of gaff from his former buddies who were part of the opposition, but Ted had grown up on a farm, had his feet on the ground, and was big, well built, soft spoken, and such criticism seemed to roll off his back. On the twelfth, my one man crew was unexpectedly augmented when Paul Hartnett, a high school teacher, and his wife Jane Piereth, then giving sailing lessons, and Jerry Borkenhagen, another neighbor, showed up in life jackets, saying they were coming along to help.

That's how it was, neighbor against neighbor, and somehow that fact never seemed to register sufficiently with newly-recruited protestors to make them ask why we were in favor of the project or for them to question their own motives or the motives of their leadership.

Of course, if they were true believers, those considerations wouldn't concern them. And that's the history and failure of all true believers. Whether fascist, communist, religious fanatics, or elitists, they all end up as thought-controlling dictatorships. Years later I was asked by a lady, one of the early opposition, why their boats hadn't been included in the plan? It was at least fifteen years after the houseboat war, and she was still thinking in terms of their propaganda. Their leadership had wanted to take over the property, and any tactics or logic or lies that served the purpose were acceptable.

Sometime before Lew Cook had leased the property—while our master plan was still in planning at the county level—I had written a short "poem" on a napkin in the No Name Bar in Sausalito after attending what I thought would be a fun party, but which had turned into be a political harangue complete with loud music presented by the leader of a local band. His schtick was to thumb his nose at all convention. He was a natural leader who was good at stirring things up, but he had a pragmatic sense that later kept him off the lines and out of trouble. The poem went as follows:

"The Problem"
Don't bore me with history's lessons or confuse me with issues and facts,
I need slogans and simply answers and leaders who don't reason but act.
I am fulfilled in the excitement of action, find comfort in following a flag.
In my time I have crucified Jesus and marched for *Grossdeutschland* rights.
I've been called patriot, pig, and the people. I'm the parent who doesn't listen and the child who's too smart to ask. I need my leaders who use me and deserve them, and best of all I get someone to hate. Problem? What problem?
You've got the problem; I'll always take the easy way.

Many years later, well after the houseboat war, some of us were at a meeting still trying to figure out a way to berth the original thirty-five protester boats in a manner that would be acceptable to the harbor, the other residents, and the bureaucracies. The fellow who had inspired my bar-napkin poem was present. He spoke up and objected to one proposal that would have positioned a few of the thirty-five boats somewhere near an already legal boat he had recently acquired. He said that the new berths as proposed would impair his views and reduce the value of his boat. Two of the guys I'd faced across the protest lines and who knew him well looked over at me, and all three of us cracked up. Our famous rebel leader had become what he had said he hated. Hypocrisy? No, just self-interest.

Monday, December 12, 1977, our little Armada started out, me towing my pile driver with deputies on floats tied alongside and other deputies in small boats going ahead. We went around the end of B-Dock from the north side and headed roughly southwest toward the D-Dock work site. The Coast Guard boat was well outboard of the property off our port bow. The protestors' fleet of small boats was spread out ahead and to the right between us and the shoreline where we had to start work, with a concentration of boats positioned to block a narrow channel between two large, grounded arks which we had to negotiate in order to reach the work site. Like the Spanish Armada, and contrary to popular myth, we were both outnumbered and outgunned. Outgunned because we didn't use missiles such a bolts, pipes, oars, two-by-fours, etc. Nonetheless we persisted and made our way through the blockade to where we were to start pile driving near the shore. At that location, butted to the end of what is now the D-Dock parking lot, there was an old one-hundred-ten-foot, three-unit houseboat on one side owned by Francis Carlough, one of our earliest residents and a good friend. On the other side of us was a temporary walkway and obstructions that could be controlled by deputies, so we were able to do our job without interferences once in position.

By the time we'd gotten through the slot between the two large, grounded arks, the deck of my little rig was littered with objects that had to be cleared in order to work. I still have a couple of long oars, which were thrown or grabbed by deputies. I'd seen one deputy felled by a bolt to the head and one protester go overboard either falling or trying to do a berserker into one of the sheriff's boats. It was all very dramatic and very loud as protestors fought boat to boat with the deputies and/or tried to board the pile driver while deputies fended off their boats with long two-by-fours and captured oars. I had locked up my two sharp pike poles in my workboat on our final approach, so they wouldn't get misused in the heat of the moment, and had tied the boat up to a friendly ark that formed one side of the slot we'd had to negotiate going in.

The noise on the twelfth of December 1977 was something like a bunch of people banging on boards with hammers and yelling at the top of their lungs. I did my best to ignore the noise and the action and concentrated on keeping the rig moving, which we did by hand. One fellow started kicking my deck hand, Ted, who was fending off from the man's houseboat by hand so we wouldn't bump it—a standard and considerate procedure. A deputy saw what was happening, chased the guy into his houseboat, and arrested him for assault. Afterwards, the kicker sued the county and, I believe, the city of Tiburon, whose officers may have been present under a mutual aid agreement, for violating his civil liberties. The Marin County district attorney (DA), instead of asserting his own position, made an economic decision to pay off the guy to the tune of $10,000, perhaps with the county's insurance, thereby validating and rewarding and encouraging the use of violence by the protestors as a means of achieving their political and economic goals. The deputy DA who was handling the case quit his county job in disgust. We felt the same way, but couldn't quit. Ironically, the fellow involved had been one of the first to sign a lease for a berth on the dock we were trying to build. He still lives there in a large valuable houseboat that he has expanded over the years.

The tide dropped, we shut down, and the protesters went home to watch themselves on television. I've often wondered what would happen if a demonstration was given, and the T.V. producers deemed it un-newsworthy, so no cameras came. Would the organizers bother to give a second showing?

Some of the deputies wondered why we quit before dark. They weren't familiar with tides. To my surprise, the deputies then also left. The county was still new to waterfront tactics, and it would cost us dearly. After securing my rig, I ran my workboat back to B-Dock and then headed to La Petite, a great soup and sandwich shop that used to be roughly behind and across the street from the Strawberry shopping center in Mill Valley. I sat there marveling at how calm and bright and normal everything seemed. I think my ears were still ringing. A friend, Ron Young, came in and sat at my table. He'd just run or practiced to run a marathon, and we talked about that. Ron, an architect, lived with his delightful wife Gil and their daughter Ami on a houseboat at Gate 6 1/2. He had chosen the plants and had drawn our landscaping plan for the BCDC design review board. Ron and Jill's home and his office are now in Mill Valley. His daughter Ami is a CPA with, I believe, her own office in San Rafael.

The next day we continued work on the pier, tying up my rig at night outboard of Fran's barge, end-to, close enough to step on or off and easy for her to keep an eye on it. All work shortly stopped, though, because early in the morning of December 15, a 110' x 32' x 9' standard, wooden, covered lighter, which years earlier had been converted to a houseboat and was once berthed at Gate 6 1/2 and used in the production of porno movies, was moved into position and sunk to plug the hole we'd come through on the twelfth. My rig was thus trapped and construction of D-Dock was stopped for the next two years and eight months.

It would be the first time, to my knowledge, that a vessel—my baby pile driver—had been successfully blockaded on American waters by the use or threat of force since the American Civil War, and despite repeated complaints and requests and written statements by eye-witnesses, no government entity with jurisdiction, including the County of Marin, the state of California, or the federal government took any action against those responsible even though the people were known and statutes and code sections had clearly been violated. Legal action by me offered no solution at all, only a sinkhole for legal fees. The best advice of one attorney was for me to sue Lew Cook as having insurance and the only easily accessible deep pockets—which I wouldn't do. Government and law enforcement in all its forms backed off and the whole problem was left in the property owner's lap, who was attempting to make improvements mandated by the same government under threats of abatement.

No politician or highly-placed bureaucrat was willing to stick his or her neck out to enforce the law against anyone associated with a well-organized mob in a very public controversy where there was no political currency to be gained. The property owner and his tenants were left to protect themselves and to deal with problems at Waldo Point with the ever-implied threat by government of withholding any future help if Lew Cook didn't go along. In effect, a property owner was being told he had to hire a private army without any of the legal protection afforded police officers acting in the line of duty, and without the right to arrest, and have to expect to pay all the legal costs predictably arising out of such an arrangement—if he wanted to protect his tenants and his rights. Because so many government officials in positions of responsibility and authority failed to act in accordance with their own rules, there was no rule-of-law at Waldo Point, only political expediency, and the webs men weaved. The property owner and his tenants, who were trying to obey the law, paid the price. It was clear that making a big noise, acting in a large group, rioting, vandalizing, burning, making threats, manipulating the press, and, being largely uncollectible, was the way to go. As Margaret Azevedo put it in a September 13, 1980 column in the *Independent Journal,* the rest of us were "The forgotten people of this saga, whose chief failing, it seems, was their adherence to those unspeakably middle-class habits of paying rent, minding the law, and counting on government to do right."

As bad as it was for Lew cook, it really didn't change anything for the rest of us, his tenants. We were used to living without the protection of law. We'd had to deal with the heroin problem by ourselves so we could also deal with the rest of it by ourselves if forced to, and if government didn't like how we did it they could always enforce the law against us, which they'd just shown they weren't up to. It was not a pretty situation.

In July of 1969, when I first got seriously involved, I'd been advised, and I believed that government had the right and the means and the duty to enforce the laws they were invoking against Arques and the houseboaters. I based my actions on that belief. However, when it got down and dirty, when push came to shove, it was no different than with the heroin. Government may have had the right and the means and the duty, but they lacked the will, and we were again left on our own. The lesson to me was that you cannot trust governments. In the absence of core values, political self-interest always rules.

Or as Arques would say, "A politician is someone who sits on the fence, talks out of both sides of his mouth, and carries water on both shoulders." Arques was right about a lot of things.

* * *

The next step for the protestors after December 12, as "the abused party," was to push for an earlier requested Marin County Human Rights Commission hearing and sue in federal court for civil rights abuses. A lot of showboating, but nothing much came of either, except maybe some useful press for the protestors by publicly accusing us of violating their civil liberties. Complaints by houseboaters against the protestors were tendered at the same time, but were neither noted nor considered by the Human Rights Commission. I think the county was just using the commission as a safely value for social gas.

On January 10, 1978, in a letter to the Marin Board of Supervisors, referring to the ongoing hearings before the Human Rights Commission, Douglas J. Maloney, Marin's County Counsel, wrote:

January 10, 1978

Board of Supervisors
Marin County Civic Center
San Rafael, California 94903
Re: Human Rights Commission
Waldo Point
Dear Supervisors:

Inasmuch as the Human Rights Commission has requested you to consider issuing of subpoenas for certain public witnesses, this seems a good time to evaluate the progress of this matter to date.

Subsequent to your request to the Human Rights Commission to review this matter, there have been a number of developments which necessarily influence any intelligent evaluation of this problem. Some of these are:

1. A barge was deliberately scuttled in an attempt to prevent construction of a pier.
2. An amended complaint has been filed in the pending lawsuit which names the Board of Supervisors individually. This amendment seeks to hold Board members <u>personally</u> liable for $5 million in compensatory and $5 million in punitive damages.
3. The Superior Court has issued an order, which, among other things, specifically finds that residents of the Marina have tried to obstruct the development by:
   (a) "Threatening <u>injury and death</u> to employees of Waldo Point Harbor" (emphasis added),
   (b) "Boarding, without permission, the pile driving rig and cutting lines thereto," and
   (c) "Engaging in violent physical combat with law enforcement personnel. . ."
      i. (The Protester's Lead Attorney) has instituted and maintained a mendacious and defamatory publicity campaign for the purpose of influencing the deliberations of the Human Rights Commission.
      ii. (DITO) has advised your Board, by letter, and made numerous media statements to the effect that residents of the Marina will resist any effort to enforce lawful court orders with violence, even if such may result in injury or death.
      iii. The contractor's office has been burglarized of papers pertaining to this matter.

All of the above have created an atmosphere in which it is difficult, if not impossible, for the Human Rights Commission to proceed in a calm and deliberative fashion guaranteed to insure a fair exposition of all sides of the controversy.

Moreover, to date, although the Commissioners have persevered with diligence and integrity, they have been unable to conduct the hearings in a manner calculated to produce a judicious decision. For example,

1. None of the Commission's rules of procedure have been regularly enforced, and most have been ignored.
2. Notwithstanding a specific provision that participation by attorneys would be limited, (theirs) has been allowed to interrupt at will, coach and correct witnesses, explain testimony, and engage in random discourse.
3. Witnesses, of whose testimony the audience does not approve, have been hooted, jeered, contradicted from the floor, and, in some cases, threatened.
4. Witnesses have not been required to testify under oath, and much of the testimony consisted of rank hearsay, speculation, and uninformed opinion.
5. The Commission staff assured our office that, prior to the testimony of public witnesses, we would be given an intelligible statement of the issues to which the Commission desired a response. This has never been accomplished, other than in a fragmentary and uninformative manner.

As a consequence, with all due respect to the Commission, we believe it is unreasonable to expect that any sound and reasoned judgment can result without some improvement in the fact-finding methods of the Commission.

To this end, I believe it would behoove the inquiry if your Board deferred consideration of the issuance of subpoenas at this time, granted the Commission an extension of time to complete their study, and recommended a respite of approximately thirty days. During this period, the Commission staff could analyze the evidence received to date, investigate the matter in detail, prepare a comprehensive summary of salient and verifiable facts, and provide County agencies with an intelligent statement of the issues yet to be considered, other than those which cannot be discussed due to pending criminal cases and the prohibitions on pre-trial publicity. Concurrently, the Commission could work with County staff to develop procedures which will insure that future hearings will be conducted impartially, with decorum.

If you wish to discuss the foregoing in greater detail, I will be pleased to assist.

Very truly yours,
Douglas J. Maloney
County Counsel
DJM:sl

One of Cyra McFadden's characters in her 1977 book about Marin County, *The Serial*, in reference to a dispute about live music in Mill Valley bars, said, "The real problem was the Human Rights Commission which seemed to believe in human rights mainly for hippies with amplifiers."

On the way back from testifying in federal court in San Jose in a related civil rights case I got rear ended by an uninsured young man who was either drunk or high. I had to tie the bumper of my VW bug to a telephone pole when I got home and pull it out so I could open the hood.

* * *

Near the end of the period when my rig was trapped, the fellow who had earlier wrapped his arms around a pile I was about to drive, approached me with a proposition. He said the protesters were willing to release my rig from the blockade so I could "get back to work." I declined the offer in view of government's conduct since the blockade started. Despite how much I would have liked to have my rig free, I reasoned that if I accepted the protesters' offer we would be back to zero with D-Dock, the protestors' position would be immeasurably improved, and we would face an even bigger fight when we tried to resume work. Probably this time without any help from the sheriff since government at that point would no doubt figure it better for Cook to "pay off" the protestors by giving them something—the D-Dock area perhaps—rather than involving itself again in the messy business of law enforcement. D-Dock would not get built, the "community organizers" would have won, and the rest of us would be screwed. My rig stayed put and D-Dock was eventually built with the sheriff's help. (I use expletives when I can't think of a group of words or a term that is more descriptive of what I am trying to convey—or when it is a direct quote.)

Throughout the period of conflict, a main thrust of the protestors' tactics seemed to have been to cost our property owner so much money in attorney's fees and security costs, that he would either quit entirely or compromise his interests—and ours—by abandoning a portion of his property to them. Burying an opponent in legal and other costs has long been a proven and popular tactic, and if you are uncollectible but have a newsworthy cause there are always idealistic, lefty, ambitious, or publicity-hungry attorneys available to work for little or nothing so long as the issue sports the correct buzzwords—in our case, starting with "People vs. The Developer." On the other hand, if you're someone who has enough assets to exceed the cost of collecting attorney's fees, justice can be very expensive. In our case, the advantage of "free" attorneys for the protestors was partly offset in favor of the property owner by his paying tenants, who backed him in every possible way.

One interesting advantage the tenants did enjoy was a limited degree—not total by any means—of safety from serious violence being attempted against us or our boats; if civilians were targeted in newsworthy numbers, the protest leadership knew that perceived public sentiment might turn against them and politicians might lose some of the spaghetti in their spines. I have no doubt that the protestors' professional "community organizers" would have preferred to see their own foot soldiers hurt, particularly a woman or child, which would have provided them with a publicity coup and a rallying cry.

Assaulting cops was okay, of course, because the protestors' media image would be poor people defending their homes against police brutality.

* * *

Before the attempt to build D-Dock, A-Dock had been driven and built and occupied, B-Dock was driven and well on its way to completion, and Main Dock, the only real dock on the property from the old days, was re-driven in place and was already occupied. Two docks to go, D and E, or Liberty and South 40, as we call them.

When long and intense legal work slowed after our D-dock failure, an event occurred that threatened to sour the relationship between Lew and his tenants. A meeting was held by some of the opposition with then sheriff, Al Howenstein, on an ark at the head of the planned South 40 pier. From there an urgent call was made to Lew Cook by Sheriff Howenstein to come to the ark and meet with them. The gist of the meeting was that Lew should forego any further attempt to build D-Dock until they, the protestors, received approvals to design and construct and manage their own area, in essence, holding D-Dock hostage until that happened. They did give their permission to proceed with E-Dock (the South 40). A short, handwritten document was drawn to that effect. It was a shift in their strategy, the new apparent target being control of the unbuilt D-Dock area. It was clear to Lew Cook that if he didn't sign the agreement, Sheriff Howenstein would not provide further protection for work in the harbor. Lew had come to the meeting alone, without his attorney or anyone else, and was being told by the chief law enforcement officer of Marin County that future law enforcement would be withheld if Lew didn't agree, then and there, to the protestors' demands. It couldn't have been clearer than that. Lew signed, and it became known as the "September 5th Agreement."

The first item of the agreement read, "Developers commitment to the Goal of Plans to accommodate the people currently on the property, anchor-outs, and Gate 3." I presume that meant those people on the property who had refused the offer of berths on the already approved docks and those who had moved onto the property since the conflict started who, in concert, had tried to invalidate the permits and prevent the rest of us from getting berths. As to the Gate 3 Marinship property, Arques had, as I recall, nineteen houseboat tenants there who had already been counted as future Waldo Point residents. Two decided to move to Galilee Harbor in Sausalito instead, and seventeen had signed up for berths on the approved docks, including a number who were waiting for the completion of D-Dock.

As already noted, Lew had been trying to accommodate all existing boats from the beginning and had never ceased the effort. Records of the period are replete with government and harbor documents to that effect. However, the protestors made clear by their actions that their goals were now different and much broader than what they had originally stated, and that they wouldn't be satisfied by what the harbor, the county, and even the BCDC were trying to do for them. The game for them was to try to gain additional concessions on top of each preceding concession until they achieved their ultimate objective, whatever that happened to be. The Russians communists taught us that one after World War II.

There was a lot of disappointment and anger when the rest of us heard about the September 5ᵗʰ Agreement. Why hadn't his tenants, particularly those who were waiting for the berths they'd signed leases for on D-Dock, at least been advised of what was afoot? What right did Sheriff Howenstein have to interfere? Wasn't his job to protect citizens from violence and unlawful destruction of property instead of using the police power of the state to dictate political decisions? After that, we saw Howenstein as just another problem instead of as a neutral law enforcement officer. When his term as sheriff was up, a sergeant in his own department, Chuck Prandi, unseated him with major support from law enforcement. Not only at Waldo Point, but elsewhere, Howenstein was seen as an aspiring politician, not a law enforcement officer. During the hunt for the Trailside Killer, according to deputies I'd spoken to, he downplayed rather than supported the kind of basic police work that solves cases in favor of the latest profiling and other exotic new methods. Reportedly, he also loved microphone and camera time. After Howenstein left office, the job he was rewarded with in Sacramento, in part, I understood, involved determining who got drug enforcement money.

In a move to follow up on their September 5ᵗʰ success, a call was made by the protestors for a meeting between Lew and their attorneys to take place on their ground in one of their offices. Lew Cook came with counsel this time, and I was also present. Their lead attorney made his pitch, mostly about all the violent people they couldn't control, who were gearing up to stop further construction and that some of them, he'd been told, had AK-47s—a revealing choice of weapons. I don't believe he mentioned that to the sheriff. His point was that it was hopeless for Lew to try to proceed and that he had to give up at least some of his property to the protestors before it was "too late." The speech was mesmerizing and depressing and cleverly calculated to make us feel hopeless and helpless in the face of it.

Then I sounded off saying that we, the other "people," had guns, too, and would be happy to accommodate them (or words to that effect). That shocked everyone, as though, "My goodness, we weren't actually threatening you!" It was obviously time for wiser heads to prevail, and all the attorneys present promptly agreed to exclude me from the rest of the meeting. I cooled my heels in the waiting room until the meeting adjourned shortly afterward. My outburst had broken the spell, though, and Lew turned them down flat, and nothing further came of it.

In retrospect, from what I'd heard and seen in that meeting in that attorney's office, I could for the first time sense how it was possible for a gangster like Hitler to browbeat a guy like Chamberlain into agreeing to stand by, while Hitler proceeded to take over Czechoslovakia, another people's country, in the name of peace.

* * *

Work on the South 40 pier proceeded with outside contractors while the rest of us labored to reverse the effect of September 5th. While all this was going on, A- and B-Docks were finished up and berths occupied by their lessees. With some minor changes, C, or Main Dock, was already occupied and had been re-built in place.

All Waldo Point Harbor residents, not just paying tenants, and also anchor-outs in county waters, at county and BCDC insistence, were from the beginning offered berths in all the newly legal harbors. Mimi Tellis hung a king-sized sheet with the words "Berths Available" printed on it in giant letters across the south end of the ferryboat City of Seattle, which was her home and office, in order to clearly give notice she was complying. I seem to recall she had two berths available that weren't occupied by existing tenants. The people who were doing their best to stop the work in our harbor already knew all about our policies, if they paid attention at all, because everything was on the table through repeated court sessions, active pamphleteering from both sides, and endless dialogue. A number of the protestors had already chosen berths and had signed leases, some, no doubt, just to cover their backsides in case they didn't prevail, and some who had signed leases had already sold out for substantial profits. All houseboat leases were renewable and, as a practical matter, good in perpetuity so long as berthage was paid. Since 1977, when Lew took over, I don't believe a boat has ever been evicted from a leased berth. On occasion, when someone got into financial trouble, they would simply sell out for a profit, and the boat stayed.

* * *

The most dangerous period of the houseboat war was near the end. A short while before we re-started work on D-Dock, a shot was fired one night through the bedroom window of Mitze Carlough—the young daughter of Fran, whose barge my rig was tied behind—missing her by a few inches and lodging in an upright piano. By then, that sort of thing was so much in keeping with the norm for our neighborhood that the deputies who responded, the next morning, didn't bother to see where the slug went. A neighbor, Joe Foley, a San Francisco building inspector, traced it, dug it out of the upright piano, and showed it to the deputies. That was the end of the investigation. The Harbor cleaned up the broken glass, put up a sheet of one-and-an-eighth-inch plywood on the wall next to Mitze's bed, and the young lady resumed its use without comment.

Someone took a shot at me late one night as I was walking on B-Dock. The slug came from the darkened Gate 6 area and passed close enough for me to clearly hear it snap as it went by my head. I walked back and forth for a while hoping there would be a second try so I could see where it came from, even though I knew I couldn't respond. I later only mentioned it to one person, a natural warrior who could passionately take any side of an argument just for the sake of fighting. It made her feel good to be against something, and I was glad she was on our side. I swore her to secrecy because I didn't want the incident to signal a further escalation in the level of violence. She kept her word.

To my knowledge, no one responsible for setting fires, shooting, sabotaging equipment, firebombing, breaking in, vandalism, or any similar nighttime activities was ever identified or prosecuted, nor am I aware of any effort to do so, particularly during the four plus years of organized violence. We did finally convince Sheriff Howenstein to assign a couple of deputies to walk the property, mostly so they could get to know us personally instead of working blind, not knowing who was who. It definitely helped.

Good beat cops on foot are probably the single best deterrent to street crime, next to alert residents, because they get to know everyone, are friendly with everyone, including children who can use good role models, and eventually everyone talks to them. Ours would periodically stop by the office on their rounds at night to get a cup of coffee or use the facilities and were not reluctant to express their opinions about the unusual restrictions under which they were required to operate. One of the deputies was ready to quit the department. I'd seen deputies assaulted during demonstrations and then ordered not to pursue and arrest, so I understood what they were talking about. When you realize that many of the police were the same age as many of the protestors, and consider all the verbal and physical abuse directed at them—enough to inflame anyone—it was a tribute to the training and professionalism of the deputies that they kept their cool. Of course, they also knew they were being deliberately baited in the hopes of getting a photo opportunity to show police violence against helpless citizens who were only exercising their "freedom of speech." Right.

Chapter 12

A Break

Eventually the protestor's plans to take over D-Dock fell apart. They moved the blockade barge, rather than losing it, and construction re-started with more protests. Sheriff Howenstein delegated the job of protection to a good man, Lieutenant Robert Doyle, who in turn was later elected sheriff of Marin County and serves in that position to this day. Lieutenant Doyle was a smart, standup guy who ignored politics, operated by the rules, and was straightforward in doing his job. This time when someone ignored a lawful order or assaulted a deputy or someone else, or was seen to commit an illegal act, that person was arrested on the spot or pursued until arrested. Then they were hauled to the Civic Center, booked, arraigned, bail set, and they had to pay up before they could get out. No more "own recognizance" and right back to the protests with no consequence for their behavior. Sheriff Howenstein was no longer seen on the property.

Lieutenant Doyle led from the front. On a low tide, I was looking for holes to patch in the wet, muddy hold of a second 110' barge the protestors had moved to Waldo Point and sunk in an attempt to duplicate the blockade barge they'd just removed, when a protestor climbed down a hatch with the intent to interrupt my work. Lieutenant Doyle saw what was happening, stuck his head in, and in a normal tone of voice told the young man to come back out or he, Lieutenant Doyle, was going to come down and arrest him. It was no bluff, and the young man was not stupid. He got right out.

When we learned later that the second 110' barge had been found adrift in San Francisco Bay by the US Army Corps of Engineers, towed to their dock in Sausalito, and was then stolen from them by the protesters, a couple of us approached a full-bird colonel at the corps and briefly laid out the problem. He picked up his phone to get confirmation of what we'd told him and then ordered someone to retrieve the stolen barge. Straightforward, no bullshit, old school. For once we went home happy. Until, that is, we arrived back at my office and got a message from the colonel that he had been ordered by his superiors to stand down and take no action to recover the barge that had been stolen from the US Army Corps of Engineers. It was left to Lew to arrange removal of the second blockade barge. Nothing had changed.

Throughout my experience at Waldo Point, government in its many forms has never operated by a consistent standard of right and wrong or justice, or even law, only, it seems, by what is expedient in terms of how its decisions might affect political comfort zones and careers. Calculations about possible short-term news reporting and public response, I'm sure, play a big part in their decisions. The bottom line seems to be to avoid problems and protect public images, which of course gives a huge advantage to the noisiest contestant in any controversy that comes before them. Nothing that government did or said or threatened or promised or enacted regarding houseboats could be believed or relied on because implementation or enforcement might became a political problem for those making the decisions. The citizens of Waldo Point who tried to live by the law and who had every right to expect it to be applied equally were unceasingly disappointed and left holding the bag. Kind of a grown-up version of a snipe hunt—being left out in the cold waiting to catch a non-existent equality under the law. Or, if you'd prefer, we were a bunch of naive and trusting Charlie Browns who had the football jerked away each time, and the government was Lucy.

* * *

The use of organized and directed violence by the protestors at Waldo Point ended shortly after we re-started construction of D-Dock and marked the unofficial end of the houseboat war. Facing serious arrest under Lt. Doyle and the knowledge that they would have to come up with bail money each time and the possible need to defend themselves in court each time, meant that organized violence had become too expensive to any longer be a productive tactic; their leadership turned it off in <u>one day</u>. I suspect, also, that some of the more well-to-do sympathizers who had been fronting bail money said, "Enough."

Not only was illegal behavior at Waldo Point no longer going to be excused just because it was done in conjunction with a group protesting something, but in the background there was also a growing awareness among the protestors that having a legal berth on the property was worth money. Cost primarily, on the one hand, what they'd tried to do to us, and the prospect of easy money combined to stop the war, and grand principles were relegated to lip service.

By the time the houseboat war ended, a number of the protestors had already signed leases and were enjoying the benefits of adequate and reliable utilities if already on a finished dock, and, in any case, a huge increase in the value of their houseboats. One of them who signed a lease early sold out for enough money to be able to buy property in Sonoma. I later ran into her in a restaurant, and she complained to me that her tenants weren't paying their rent, which made it hard for her to pay her mortgage and meet her other obligations. I guess that is what's called a learning curve. One fellow sent a letter to me from Paris asking me to collect rent from his tenants on his houseboat, for which he wasn't paying and hadn't paid any berthage, so he could stay in Paris a little longer. I didn't respond.

During that later period, Lew contracted with a man who could provide a crew of Samoan security guards. Lew had tried a number of security companies with poor or indifferent results. Most guys employed in that business, since they had no personal stake in our affair, were not eager to put their butts on the line for what they were being paid. They served mostly as eyes. There was one gentleman, though, a Sikh from a long tradition of warriors, complete with blue turban, who was a jewel. He couldn't have weighed more than 125 pounds and was poorly paid, but he took his charge seriously. He would call the office late at night on radio checks, and in his Indian/English accent proudly announce, "My eyes are open and my hand is on my gun." That always got a laugh (military humor) and brightened our day.

The Samoans, unlike other outfits, were a clannish lot, had their own language, which was great for communication security, and you didn't' mess with one without taking on all of them. They moved into the old Addington ark, so they always had immediate backup available for their guys on guard duty. The protestors, never bashful in their choice of tactics, at one point tapped the phone line to the Addington ark.

Resident volunteers continued to take care of A and B-Docks. Main Dock wasn't a problem since some of the protestors lived on Main Dock, had leases, and weren't going to burn themselves out. That left only D-Dock and the South 40 for the Samoans to watch.

The Samoans had a knack for playing by protestor rules. When the Harbor was sued for something the Samoans had supposedly done, they could never be found for subpoenas, couldn't be questioned because no one could speak their language, or prove they also spoke English, and besides, they didn't know anything about it, it was someone else. I loved it, and I suspect by then the judges found it amusing too. In one instance, a Samoan of unusually slight stature was attacked late at night by one of the protester's harder types, an ex-con and his friends, which brought out everyone, and the fight was on. It wasn't one of those Marin deals where nobody is seriously hurt and everybody quits at five to go home and watch themselves on television. This was a genuine rumble. No media were present, and the other side didn't do so well. Of course, the Harbor was sued and when it got to court, with no Samoans present, and their chief witness with bruises and wired jaw complained of ill treatment, the judge almost laughed him off the stand. The days of knee-jerk sympathy were over. The judge called it mutual combat and dismissed the suit.

* * *

By the restart of D-Dock construction, the media had also pretty much lost interest in us. We were told we were "no longer newsworthy." That was fine with us since so much of the coverage had only served to inspire further protest. At the beginning, the majority of the media coverage had been so one-sided that a large group of paying tenants called their own press conference in order to make most reporters aware that there were people on the property besides protesters; residents who actually wanted the place cleaned up and wanted to become legal. I even engineered a fake rent strike demanding that the project continue. Nearly every paying tenant on the property wrote a letter to Lew Cook to that effect, care of me, and yet not a dime of rent was actually withheld. I don't think I ever showed the letters to Lew, but held them to prove the point to the press or whoever when useful. Of course, we had no intention of making life any harder for Lew than it already was and knew we'd just be hurting ourselves if we cut off any of the funds he needed to fight our war. The rent strike helped Lew somewhat by making politicians pay attention to Lew's tenants. I'm sure they feared that the houseboat problem could still be thrown back into their laps.

In what turned into a contest for the best publicity, we made sure that the phony rent strike received enough coverage to get us on the map. Some of Lew's limited partners took it so seriously they wanted Lew to get rid of me. When they saw that no money was withheld and recognized the benefits, they backed off. My goodness, was no one interested in the facts? Much later, after the September 5ᵗʰ Agreement was signed, a real rent strike was threatened by D-Dock leaseholders. If it had been necessary to go through with it, most of the regular tenants in the harbor would have joined the strike in sympathy.

Part of the reason the press lost interest in our affair was Bob Kallock. Bob was the first live-aboard anchor-out in Richardson Bay on something other than a yacht. His basic philosophy was to live as simply as possible so his time would be his own, but he never knocked or belittled anyone else's choices. He'd grown-up in New England in a tradition of town hall democracy, knew the electrical trade, had sailed in the Military Sea Transport Service (MSTS) during Vietnam, and was one of the first of my acquaintances to acquire and master computers. Bob Kallock was one of our community elders. You had to put on the brakes when talking to him, though, because he considered his words carefully before speaking and then what he said was intelligent, insightful, and to the point. His standing was such that he had the respect of both sides during the houseboat war even though he had verbally and physically supported what I had been doing from the start.

As I recall, only one person publicly badmouthed Bob Kallock, in a letter in mid-1977, referring to a statement Bob had made that was quoted in a newspaper article. The letter writer accused Bob of being a "Quisling,"ⁱᵛ of being an associate of mine, of not even being a resident of Waldo Point, and of being promised a choice berth in exchange for the statement quoted in the newspaper. (What? The writer thought some of the approved berths were good!) At the time, Bob Kallock was in charge of most of the houseboat berthing in Arques's Marinship harbor and also lived there. He had, much earlier, before Waldo was leased to Lew Cook, helped me make Marinship houseboaters aware of their priority for the planned berths at Waldo Point and get them signed up on a waiting list. Before I met Lew, I was concerned that the Marinship houseboaters might be left out if they didn't have a paper trail.

After Lew took over the harbor, Bob helped me with the follow up to get them their leases. Bob and another mutual close friend, Patrick Vaughan, moved their small houseboats—one built on a thirty-six-foot LCVP and the other on a thirty-six-foot LCPL—from Marinship to A-Dock as soon as it was ready for occupancy in order to help with security.

Patrick Vaughan was a native of San Francisco, a World War II navy veteran of the war in the Pacific, had worked in shipyards, been a San Francisco fireman, and held a teacher's credential with a master's degree. Arques called him a "hotheaded Irish free soiler." Patrick loved Franklin D. Roosevelt, hated republicans, and at the same time had no patience at all with the young freeloaders and outsiders who were trying to bring down our community in the name of "the people." And, Patrick babysat my son when my son was very young. Patrick died in 2006 just before his ninety-third birthday. Both Bob and Patrick also helped guard the harbor office for four years without pay, and Bob continued to manage a portion of Marinship for Arques until all the houseboaters there who'd signed up for berths at Waldo got one. A few years ago, Bob had to sell his small houseboat because of his asthma and moved with his dear wife Laurabell to the dry air on the east side of the Sierras. They visit from time to time.

In dealing with the media, one of Bob Kallock's methods was to stand next to a reporter who was observing the action and slowly and patiently identify who was who and explain their relationship to what was happening. Most reporters eventually slowed down long enough to listen and most thereafter lost faith in "the people's cause" as they considered the situation with newly informed eyes. It took Bob almost two years of constant effort to adequately get everyone's attention, but then what he said stuck—that, re-enforced by the reporter's personal observations and experience with the protestors over time. After one pep rally on the barge that was blocking the construction of D-Dock, to which the press was invited, Jack Vietz, a well-known *Chronicle* reporter, was overheard by Bob Poppit saying, "We've created a monster," referring to statements made by the protestors' lead attorney.

I also recall an early, brief television interview Dean Jennings had set up on his own shortly after I'd taken over management and the media smelled a story. Dean urged me to participate, and the interviewer, a local television news personality, asked me, "But where can they go?" He was referring, I suppose, to those who were claiming they would be kicked out if we cleaned up the place. It was the only question I was asked, and I replied something to the effect, "How about where they came from?" It wasn't what he wanted to hear and that ended the interview. It was the start of the media's "poor people losing their homes" routine and of course had nothing at all to do with the reality of what had already taken place or what was occurring or whether anyone would actually be made homeless —a term that hadn't arrived yet— or who "they" were, or what kind of resources they had available, or why they were here in the first place, or what lifestyle they'd chosen. I also recall he didn't offer to house any of "them" in his home, which I'm sure had lots of rooms. The typical media approach in the early coverage was simply to ask questions that stirred the controversy. It seemed that most reporters already had their minds and their stories made up anyway and only needed some names, dates, and quotes to fill in the blanks.

* * *

Lew Cook naturally brought his own staff with him when he leased the property, so thereafter my responsibility was mostly on-site administration, tenant communication, some security, and politics with the continued and inspired help of my longtime secretary, Shirley Flack, an English woman who was very much like Michael Wormun in that nothing fazed her. She had been a child in London during the blitz, had run a business, had traveled, and was sharp as a tack. When she moved to the waterfront the first houseboat she bought was a rundown trailer on an equally rundown Styrofoam float. She fixed it up, sold it for a profit, and went on from there, becoming a prolific owner-builder and eventually graduated to remodeling and selling houses on land.

Aside from my other responsibilities, I spent a lot of time in court in harbor-related matters, and worked at my trade when I could or when required for the harbor. Ted Rose, who had built most of the Kappas houseboat harbor, including East and West Piers and Gate 61/2, was hired by Lew to be the superintendent of construction for Waldo Point Harbor. Ted Rose had not only done it all once before—we started work in the Kappas harbor in 1975—but was also experienced in all phases of construction including major plumbing and electrical work, fill, paving, and landscaping. He brought to the job a get-things-done attitude without the emotional baggage of right and wrong that I carried. It was what the job needed. He was also sensitive enough to learn and not ignore individual histories.

When I resigned as harbor master, effective March 1, 1981, judging I'd completed what I'd set out to do back in July 1969, that is, secure a permanent home for our houseboats and arks on the Arques Waldo Point property, Ted Rose took over my job and continues in that position today.

Chapter 13
Process, Politics, and Review

The stance of the Harbor and most of the regular tenants had never changed regarding what we saw as the future for our rowdies. We always assumed that at some point, right or wrong, their boats, at least the original thirty-five, would eventually be accommodated on the property. To that end we proposed anew that an additional dock be built for them in their original location, just south of B-Dock, behind the Charles Van Damm. The county backed us and hired a consultant, Matthew C. Guthrie, who redrew the 1977 Retondo Plan into a package of three proposals, which was adopted by the county board of supervisors on February 24, 1981 and became known thereafter as the Guthrie Plan. The BCDC shot it down saying it was an inappropriate use of trust property since it involved underwater streets, as though we weren't already using such property via our lease exchange. That kind of solution was stalled for many years.

Some core tenants were so disillusioned and bitter about what protestors had done and were doing and what government was and wasn't doing and the whole namby-pamby response to violence at Waldo Point that they opposed any accommodation whatsoever. If I hadn't felt it would be a wasted effort, I might have joined them, partly because I believed that having to accept the consequences of one's actions is the quickest way to grow up. However, I also felt, in fairness, that if consequences were to be doled out, government, which in my view bore the lion's share of responsibility for everyone's problems, should get its share, and I knew that just wasn't going to happen. Politicians almost never acknowledge or take responsibility for their mistakes, except sometimes after they get caught with their hand in the cookie jar or in someone else's bed and then only for damage control.

I am reminded of a professor I had, an old style democrat, who once told us that everything government does creates incentives and dis-incentives that alter the affairs of men, often with unexpected and frequently negative results, which government then usually tries to correct (often with more aberrant results) rather than admitting the error in the first place and backing off entirely.

As it has evolved, we have a special class of citizens among us today at Waldo Point, recipients of a patronizing variety of concessions, subsidies, and entitlements. The only required qualification being that they were members of the original protest group or successors in ownership. It is interesting to note that most already have expensive concrete barges, which is a good trick for a "poor" person in a still illegal houseboat for which permits and normal financing are not yet available.

My gut feeling is that government, whatever its altruistic or self-serving motivation, has done a disservice to some here who might have gotten on with their lives if they'd had a clear yes or no answer early, instead of wasting their energies for years like Dickens's *Bleak House* characters, waiting for the resolution of a very long legal process. In Dickens's story, the characters' agonies finally ended when the lawyers drained the estate in question, and there was nothing left to fight over. In Dickens's story (and ours), it was really time that was drained from their lives, and in our case, the damage was compounded because as long as the protestors lived in limbo, their drug culture was not only ignored, but, in effect, shielded by government's involvement; and thus allowed to persist with all its inherent problems and casualties. In the end, the county's solution to the remaining drug problem at Waldo Point was to change its name to low-income housing and subsidize it, what has sometimes been referred to as our government-sponsored, tax-supported criminal sanctuary.

Except for one valiant try by "Sergeant" Prandi (who unseated Sheriff Howenstein) in a July 30, 1984 raid in the undeveloped Gate 6 area where most of the protestors lived, nothing was ever done by government about drugs at Waldo Point, nor was anything ever done about the remaining health and safety issues that were supposedly the reasons for all the hullabaloo in the first place. The July thirtieth raid by Prandi resulted in sixteen arrests and a July 30, 1984 quote in the *Independent Journal,* "car loads of high school kids stop to purchase drugs." One might conclude from government's inaction at Waldo Point that illegal drugs and the people whom those drugs affected were, or are, not important enough to deserve their attention, and also that there are no more health or safety issues here because surely something would have been done about them during the succeeding years besides talk if health and safety were actually a concern.

Other than the lack of proper sewage disposal, it appears that what drove the county actions at Waldo Point was the incorrect appearance of the place and, of course, the institutional desire to bring everything under a uniform standard that makes each unit and each owner easier to identify for the purpose of taxation. And, incidentally, makes insurance and financing possible which boosts values (and costs) and increases tax revenues. Possibly laudable goals, but which ignore, discourage, and even criminalize owner-built and paid for structures that are truly "affordable," low-cost homes, free of government, which, like with many of our forebears on the frontier, was our community's original appeal (along with living on the water of course).

* * *

There has definitely been a disconnect between the politicians and bureaucrats who soak up our tax money and the lives of the governed at Waldo Point. As of August 1, 2011, Waldo Point Harbor has been in a "planning process" for forty-two years, and we are not through yet. It seems to me that a government that can't make decisions and act in a timely manner ceases to be relevant to the governed and is only a useless figurehead, a distraction, and an unnecessary and wasteful consumer of resources.

For forty-two years, government's concern and law enforcement at Waldo Point has been focused on land use, planning, and codes directed at the property owners and the collectable residents. By comparison, with the one exception of Sergeant Prandi's effort on July 30, 1984, government ignored the existence of a drug problem at Waldo Point. In fact the opposite occurred. The drug culture in our community was raised to the status of a special class and has been rewarded with gifts of money and property and has been exempted from the codes, the degree of taxation, and the norms of conduct expected of the rest of us.

To my knowledge, no one's life has been ruined or lost, nor has tragedy ever struck at Waldo Point because someone, for instance, used two-by-fours in a stud wall instead of two-by-sixes, and yet that is the sort of thing that has merited all of government's attention. If government's objective has been to insure that properties and structures look slick and are as expensive as possible, thus raising property values and in turn property taxes, and to be able to do their government jobs with the least expenditure of effort—and it must be so because that has been the result—then government has succeeded admirably.

It does seem, though, in fairness, that if someone can be threatened with legal action for not conforming to a zoning ordinance or a building code—almost always victimless crimes—then it would be appropriate to at least give equal attention to the sale and use of illegal drugs, which in the end generate nothing but victims. And, yes, I understand that efforts in that direction drain rather than generate tax revenues so government has no immediate self-benefiting incentive to act so long as the drug problem stays relatively under the radar. The whole thing, though, does underline the question of just who is our government serving?

* * *

There have been two houseboat moratoriums at Waldo Point. The first was on the construction or importation of houseboats into Marin County waters enacted by the county early in the affair, but only enforced against collectible citizens. The second, shortly after Lew Cook took over the property from Arques, was a self-imposed, six-month moratorium by Lew Cook on the leasing of houseboat berths to new people; in order that existing boats in county waters, both on and off the property, could have first crack at the berths, including the boats whose owners, by word and deed, had made it crystal clear that they not only didn't want a legal berth in an approved harbor, but didn't want anyone else to have one either.

The county and BCDC were bent on getting all houseboats into the approved harbors, and the houseboat harbor owners were delegated for the task regardless of any prior financial or other relationships between them and those to whom they were required to offer the berths. This was all despite the blatant unfairness it often represented to those who had paid their share all along and made the legal berths, and our future, possible. With the standing threat of withholding police protection and having veto power over any possible plan changes the property owners might need, government got its way.

As supplicants in a planning process, property owners are to a large extent at the mercy of the discretionary powers of government, which ran to extremes in our case. A property owner's recourse is to sue, which is very expensive, uncertain in its outcome, and can stop or slow a project for years, also very expensive. The net result seems to be that whoever in government represents the current political need or the current fashion in visual, social, or physical planning ends up dictating the end product if for no other reason than the high cost of asserting one's rights under the law.

The county's moratorium on construction and importation of new houseboats into county waters is probably still on the books gathering dust. Lew's self-imposed, six-month moratorium on leasing berths to outsiders ended with the pressing need to generate income from berths not already chosen in order to help with the extraordinary legal and security costs. As a result, most of the space that had been offered to the protestors was made available and filled by new residents.

One of those who had originally refused a berth sued to get one after they'd been leased, basing his right on the priority set earlier by government. Seeing it was going to be a recurring theme, since a leased berth by then was worth a lot of money, I spoke to Allen Pendleton, later executive director of BCDC, and he consented to testify on our behalf. He reiterated on the stand my position that the property owner had acted in good faith and should not have to hold berths open indefinitely for people who had refused them when offered. We won the case and the right of the owner to exercise some control over his property. We also avoided a flood of similar suits from those who now saw profit for themselves in the project they had tried to scuttle.

It's perhaps instructive to repeat here that Lew Cook does not sell berths, he leases them. Leaseholders can then ask anything they want for the boat occupying their berth. In many cases, the value of the leasehold represents a major portion of the purchase price, space on the water being the object of the purchase, not necessarily the vessel that occupies the space. It was common in the beginning for an old boat with a lease to be purchased, a new lease issued, which could "not be unreasonably withheld," the old boat wrecked out, and a new boat built to occupy the space either to live on or for resale. The "not be unreasonably withheld" clause was put in our leases so nobody could be "frozen out"—everyone would have something to sell if they chose not to stay. We even set up a tiered rent formula that created an incentive for first-time buyers of old boats.

* * *

Al Aramburu was our supervisor during a good part of the houseboat war. Some of us had supported him when he ran for the Third District supervisor's seat, thinking he would be our best bet, but I developed mixed feelings over time. I've always liked him personally and respect his political acumen. He was smart, his word good, and he knew how to return a favor, and was great at covering his political backside and negotiating deals.

The downside, from my perspective, was his, by no means unusual, reluctance to meet certain problems, namely ours, head on. In order to avoid being sucked into the middle of our little civil war, he spent a good deal of his time, purportedly to define anchorages with an eye to getting rid of anchor-outs in Richardson Bay, promoting and almost singlehandedly creating a new layer of government: the Richardson Bay Regional Agency.

He brought Mill Valley, Sausalito, Tiburon, and Belvedere into what was essentially a Marin County problem centered in the protected waters of Waldo Point Harbor, known for its easy shore access, space for parking, bonfires, and tribal gatherings to amplified music. Al, in my opinion, kept his nose clean at the expense of Lew Cook and his tenants. What Al finally did do after the berths the protesters had repeatedly been offered and had repeatedly refused, and that had then been leased to others, was negotiate a deal in which Lew Cook was required to agree to turn over some of his remaining unplanned property to the protesters—subject to them obtaining future permits—in exchange for the "right" to finish the project originally mandated by the county under threat of abatement.

As it has evolved, the protestors will get berths for the original thirty-five (plus a few), and Lew will keep his property, the same result we could have achieved early in 1977. If Al foresaw that result, and he probably did, then here's to him.

* * *

The end of overt violence in 1981 marked an intensification of the planning exercise by the harbor and residents to try to achieve the same thing that the owner, the residents, the county, the BCDC, and the protestors had agreed to in principal during the 1977 meeting in the Gate 5 restaurant. If we had been able to proceed then, that is, to achieve the protestor's originally stated goal of staying together where they were instead of choosing berths on the already approved docks, the whole thing could have been handled with a simple plan amendment, adjustment of the street lease and some code changes, with no war, no interruption to everyone's lives, and no huge expense.

Instead, as of August 1, 2011, forty-two years after I entered the planning process on behalf of Arques, the Waldo Point Harbor still does not have the actual building permits necessary to make the minor changes necessary to formally accommodate the last thirty-five plus boats, the same thing we were talking about in 1977.

During the beef, by their count, the number of protestors' boats in our area had increased from the original thirty-five to 115 and then down to seventy-eight at the end. As it became clear that the harbor would get rebuilt despite the protestors' actions, their numbers had steadily shrunk as many lost interest and drifted off (no pun intended). Seventy-eight more boats, though, were clearly more than government was willing to accept as additional density, and of course government wasn't willing to do anything themselves to reduce that number so, again, Lew Cook was stuck with the problem, which included many, if not most, of the boats which were in fact on un-leased county "streets."

Much like the DA who'd decided to pay off the man who assaulted my deck hand during the December 12, 1977 riot, but for different reasons and without dangerous consequences, Lew made the decision to offer to buy out some of the extra boats. This was done with the knowledge and cooperation of the leadership of the late protestors who helped select those who should go and who could stay, now that it was their deal that was on the table. Lew also paid them to wreck out some of the purchased boats. Not bad. You create a problem and then get paid to solve it.

Many of the boats Lew bought out had been built or moved into the area as part of the numbers game during the houseboat war, and their owners, for various reasons, had no real attachment to the place. Under the circumstances, Lew's best option was to pay off some of them, with the cooperation of their buddies, rather than trying to evict them from county property, which Lew couldn't legally do and the county was unwilling to do.

Having to buy off some of the protestors occurred at the same time the regular collectable tenants were not only paying berthage fees, but also being required to conform to building codes and be inspected before being allowed to hook up to the new facilities. Reasonable in itself under the existing law, but part of a long-running pattern and history of unequal enforcement of the Marina and Houseboat ordinances and the McAteer-Petris Act that continues to this day.

The extortionary power of government over a citizen's use of his property, when an applicant must rely on the good will of politicians, planners, and bureaucrats, leaves few options but to go along, unless the applicant has very deep pockets with which to litigate and, in Lew's case, would have been willing to risk leaving his tenants and investors dangling in the wind.

The super-agency BCDC has even projected its power and guaranteed its jobs indefinitely into the future by placing a new twenty-year time limit on the Harbor's latest BCDC permit, which expires on March 18, 2024, unless the property owner, five months prior to expiration, submits a complete application for a new BCDC permit for renewal (and thereafter in five-year increments). It's all ostensibly in the name of public trust and public good, but that is a buzzword fiction. One can't help observing that if all of government didn't have the equipment to deal with a relatively minor drug culture in the '60s and '70s and '80s and '90s, etc., how in the world would the BCDC now propose to enforce a negative ruling against an entire well-established and now affluent community, part of which is subsidized by government itself with our tax money. An army of attorneys on both sides would raise their hands to heaven and sing hallelujah if they tried.

At this point the only practical explanation for the BCDC clinging to houseboats is a desire to justify its existence, maintain an image of power, extract additional mitigation fees, and/or continue to impress their special interest backers. And, it's all done under the worn premise that houseboaters and houseboat harbor owners are the cause of enduring problems, are not to be trusted or to be treated with respect or accorded the rights of ordinary citizens, and must be constantly monitored, except, of course, for the special class among us who are rewarded, pampered, and subsidized, and guess which residents pay for it all?

Or, perhaps, BCDC's stance toward us is just to mask the fact of BCDC's duty, under their own rules, to have acted to correct matters here in a timely manner years before. The maxim that the first obligation of politicians—including career bureaucrats—is to stay in power is alive and well in the Bay Area.

In addition, at this point, they would have to justify our removal with their own environmental impact report (EIR) because every pile and float and houseboat hull and utility and mooring line that touches the water has become a nursery and home for barnacles, shellfish, nudibranchs, crabs, worms, etc., all of which in turn provide the banquette ingredients for fish, other crabs, birds, raccoons, sea otters, and, indirectly, seals. Like old ships and other objects that are painstakingly prepared and deliberately sunk at great expense to create artificial reefs that become homes for marine creatures, our neighborhood has become a haven for marine life and a popular stop on the aquatic food chain. Shame on anyone who tries to disturb it or us. In fact, every morning grateful seagulls stand atop mooring piles and squawk, "Sanctuary much!"

* * *

Lew Cook was forced to pay for an "independent" environmental impact report in order to accommodate the last boats whose owners had refused berths under our original permits. The first draft agreed with the solution we had advocated since 1977, a form of the Retondo Plan we'd used as the basis for the 1977 discussion at the Gate 5 restaurant and which all parties at the time had agreed to in principal, but now wasn't what the BCDC wanted to hear. The BCDC staff got tangled in a backroom fight with the county planning staff, eventually got their way, and the final draft of the "independent" EIR was unloved by everyone except the BCDC.

That, two part, seven-and-three-quarter inch thick environmental impact report, dated May 1997 and 2001, cost Lew more hundreds of thousands of dollars, while the only decision that was actually addressed for the protestors' boats, which were already in the harbor, had been for years, and would be in the future, was where in the harbor their new berths would be. Hardly an environmental issue. There was not, nor had there ever been, a serious intention by government to eliminate those boats, which was the only other possibility.

Moving existing boats around in a harbor is properly a planning exercise for a harbor owner, with a nod from the local planning and building inspection departments. Simple. The EIR would have been a joke if it hadn't cost so much money and wasted so much of everybody's time.

Chapter 14

Consequences

So, what has changed on the property after all this time and expense since Lew Cook took over and the houseboat war started in 1977?

Nothing much really.

Our original county and BCDC-approved plan showed 265 houseboats and twenty arks, including the three ferryboats, for a total of 285 units. Our latest BCDC permit is for 232 regular houseboats, thirty-eight subsidized boats, three berths for ark replacements, and our nine remaining arks, for a total of 282 units—a net change of three less units of density from our original approvals. The three historic ferryboats that were lost are not being replaced with berths. Twenty-four of the protestor boats will go on a new dock a little south of where it was proposed in 1977, the rest elsewhere in the harbor.

People still come to our part of the waterfront to see houseboats, not to see bare, open water—better places for that—and not to see the design-reviewed landscaping or sit on regulation size benches, and most pedestrians and bicyclists still use the streets and parking areas instead of the formally designed paths.

What has happened at Waldo Point is that residents have grown old and died, while others have been born and grown up. Some of them have had their own children while we waited for government to either approve the necessary minor changes to our little project in order to formally accommodate the boats on the property whose owners had originally refused berths or to say "no" and proceed with abatements. They have done neither. Instead, our neighborhood became a thirty-five-acre rice bowl for bureaucrats, attorneys, planners, and consultants. And if you challenge government on any particular, that's okay, it gives them something more to talk about. We are pork chops to government, and the media can always use us on a slow news day.

Since I got involved in 1969, we have been through eight Third District Marin County supervisors—one for twelve years—four executive directors of the BCDC, four county sheriffs, and countless staff members and have dealt with attorneys and senior planners who weren't even born when we started. A disinterested observer could easily conclude that our government, particularly the BCDC, which asserts it only acts "in the public interest and for the public good," is in fact self-serving or, just as bad, hopelessly dysfunctional. I say the former is the case and the latter is the result.

The Golden Gate Bridge was funded and built; World War II, Korea, and Vietnam were fought; and we put a man on the moon in less time than Waldo Point Harbor has spent in "planning." I would argue that it is extortion to force us to pay for something we don't need in order to keep the people who are extorting the money from us in business. In other venues I believe that is called "a protection racket." No wonder our country is in such a financial mess.

* * *

So, who won the houseboat war? As happens with most conflicts, there are unintended and unexpected results. The County of Marin got houseboats off their collective desk and was able, at the end, to comply with a state mandate to "create" some "affordable" housing, all at a relatively low cost, and got a big boost in real and personal property taxes from our area. The original houseboaters, if they lived long enough and stayed, have gotten close to an ethereal and, it turns out, empty and meaningless "legal" status for their boats, but at a high cost.

It has to be noted that, in defiance of and despite the BCDC, the County of Marin wisely and continuously conducted business as usual, that is, issued building and occupancy permits for houseboats since 1977 when Lew Cook took over, thus making insurance and financing available for the houseboats that were to fill empty berths. Without that, the local houseboat projects and therefore the "cleanup" would have been hamstrung, and the county knew it.

As for the BCDC, they got a job that has lasted since 1969, but that's about it. Except for a loss of parking for the law-abiding residents, superior parking for the protestors, and a very small decrease in density, little has changed from our original county approvals. The BCDC certainly didn't improve water views or public access. They were already planned for, are matters of taste anyway, and are here regardless of the physical layout.

How about those who tried to kill the project for everyone? They got to stay, which was never really in doubt. In the meantime, for years—since way before we were even in the planning process—they paid less property taxes than the rest of us (if any at all) for a very long time, no escaped taxes, and paid less (if any for some) berthage than the rest of us. In the future, they get to continue to pay less berthage than the rest of us; get design, construction, and new housing in some cases (free or at dramatically reduced cost); will have more adequate parking than the rest of us (provided for by the Buck Fund); and in general will continue to be treated as a privileged, special class. In terms of what it has cost and what it will cost to live on a houseboat in Marin County waters, they have clearly won more than anyone else, though, with possibly one minor catch. In order to get all the special deals, they will have to surrender a degree of their personal freedom when they submit to the government control that goes with all the "free" money, assuming those conditions are enforced, a big if.

Is that what "human rights over property rights" means? Is that what being "free spirits" and "self sufficient" means? Selling out to Big Brother in exchange for a piece of one's freedom? If that sort of thing doesn't mean anything to them anymore then they came out of all this just fine, and it confirms that being militant really pays in a class-obsessed culture of guilt-ridden affluence, where nobody is held responsible for their actions and Big Brother is expected to take care of everyone, so long as enough of us pay enough taxes to support the system, including hiring enough bureaucrats to do the job. Wasn't it Margaret Thatcher who said, "The problem with socialism is that eventually you run out of other people's money"?

Most at Waldo Point who are considered "poor" by Marin standards are not the traditionally disadvantaged one normally associates with the word poor. With us, it's either a function of normal human differences, i.e., age, abilities, experience, attitudes, interests, willingness to work, and the many choices we make throughout our lives and the responsibility attached to those choices—real diversity—the things that make each of us uniquely us, or it's a deliberately chosen "lifestyle," what locals refer to as being "elective poor." Being elective poor in this country is made possible largely by the overflow from our prosperous society, and there's nothing wrong with it. By the same token, if someone really has to scrabble for food and shelter, I don't believe they would select "poor" as a lifestyle. In fact, I've never met anyone who was really poor who didn't want to be rich or at least comfortable, which is certainly possible in this country for anyone who is willing to assert themselves to learn, work, and earn it, and if they don't succeed, certainly their children can.

I remember one fellow in Sausalito from when I was new to the area who worked when he had to, lived cheaply, maintained his own vehicle, and spent the rest of his time boozing, chasing girls, partying, and otherwise enjoying life. He was once described to me by a guy I was working with as having been all his life where the other guy had been working all his life to get. So who was poor?

One does wonder about government's motivation in all of this. Has all the largesse directed at the protestors simply been an inducement to placate them? Or, as waterfront types would say, a payoff to shut them up?

Or, is there a real concern by government that those who have lived here, in their own houseboats, all of which were owner built, some for over forty years, who conducted protests for years, directed attorneys and legal actions, created and printed their own advertising and newsletters, who were master fundraisers giving concerts and other affairs to raise money, who successfully manipulated the press, who conducted effective propaganda and disinformation campaigns to promote the idea that they were (are) the beautiful people—their adoption of the historic ferryboat *Charles Van Damm* as a representative icon being a recent example, omitting the fact their original group, by playing dog in the manger, were directly responsible for its loss, as well as the loss of ferryboats *Issaquah* and *San Rafael,* all three of which were included in the approved master plan—who have dealt for years with the property owner and multiple government and private agencies, that those smart, savvy, politically astute people—that group, those individuals—are somehow incapable of caring for themselves?

If that is the standard by which we determine who needs help in our society, then government itself should be in a skilled nursing facility because the "beautiful people" who started as young, fit, and often well educated—really an advantaged class—have danced rings around government for years.

Or, is calling them low-income just bureaucrat–speak to help justify our latest plan approval? Or, God forbid, is all this just a way for professional do-gooders to feel warm and fuzzy and justify jobs? Is government actually going to monitor and audit those who belong to this "special class" and evict them or force them to sell out at a dictated price to another "poor" person if they cease to fit an artificial class profile or if they already have too much wealth or become too successful financially? Does it mean they are required to become and remain dependents of government (taxpayers) and be forced to accept subsidies in order to be able to continue to live at Waldo Point on the houseboats they already own outright and have occupied for so many years?

There is definitely an irrational element in this floating bedroom farce.

Best for our rowdies to have full rights and full responsibilities like every other citizen.

Generally speaking, if individuals are treated like responsible adults and expected to act like responsible adults, they will be responsible adults. On the other hand, if they are pandered to, watch out! Many in the rest of the harbor were low-income, got leases, did just fine, and never asked for a handout. And, if big money was needed for improvements to a boat, re-payable HUD loans have always been available to those who don't qualify for conventional financing. So the questions remain: Why the big push to throw money at this "special group," and why aren't they being dealt with as individuals like the rest of us?

It appears to me that government traps itself by its mistakes and indecisiveness into treating people who cause problems as being special in order to justify their own actions, and then it naturally follows that government must subsidize such people as proof of that justification. Kind of like Congress in dealing with the 2008 financial melt down?

Government and many of the "special class" in our story have a lot in common. You might even say they enjoy a symbiotic relationship. They depend on each other and both live off the people in the middle, those who do most of the productive work, support themselves, and contribute to the greater good. The two ends of our society definitely require watching, lest, like the ancient Greek and Roman empires, the two ends become so big they suck the life out of the middle.

What always got me about our gang, those who actually lived here, was that most weren't socialists or communists or any kind of "ists." Quite the opposite. They didn't want anyone telling them what they could and couldn't do. In that sense, they were classic Americans. They certainly wouldn't have tolerated the "State" controlling everything, and they would have been the first to the barricades if they'd been told they couldn't own their boats and cars or buy real property or how much or what they could do with it.

Generally, their style was to just take whatever the system was silly enough to offer for nothing, rely on the system to protect their rights, and then reject anything that didn't appeal to them. (Although, as Reggie Perrin supposedly said on one of his shows, "The problem with living for the moment is that it buggers up the next moment.") Indeed, they were mostly just young people taking advantage of wishy-washy adults. In terms of narrow self-interest, perfectly understandable. Unfortunately, they ignored the fact that the same system that protected their rights also protected the rights of the other boat owners and the rights of the property owners where they were freeloading.

I'm sure most recognized intellectually or maybe instinctively that property in all its forms is wealth and therefore power. And being aware, as James Madison wrote, that men are not angels, they were also aware that the right of individual citizens to own and control property is essential if there is to be any personal, economic, and political freedom rather than ownership and/or control being held exclusively by a central authority; which, ironically, they seemed to be advocating for their small group. What they definitely weren't clear on was the concept of their rights ending where the other fellow's rights begin, or that the use of force, as fun as it may have been, was a slippery standard by which to resolve differences instead of being guided by laws enacted under our Constitution. In that respect, their leadership adopted the mantle of any want-to-be dictator seeking to control property and people by whatever means are available. And control by a central authority does require a dictatorship in order to keep human beings in line, who invariably chafe and rebel under such limitations and restrictions.

Of course the most chilling threat to our personal freedom, which affects all of us, is the ever-creeping taxation and regulation of citizen's income and property by government—the easiest snatch of all. Regulation and taxation, often done with good intentions, is a perfect example of "The Salami Theory of World Domination," where you take a little slice here and a little slice there, which nobody really gets angry enough to do anything about, until you get to the end, and nobody is supposed to fight over the string. There are those in government today who believe that the rest of us human beings, we citizens, aren't the best ones to run our own lives, unlike the framers of our Constitution, who with their collective knowledge of ancient and contemporary history, were more afraid of, and had rebelled against, unrestrained government. The "elite" among us today who think they know what is best for everyone know all about salami slicing, and as a nation, our colleges graduate thousands of potential slicers every year. At Waldo Point, we've experienced over forty-two years of the local variety, and those of us who have lived through it are not impressed.

In the big picture, the protestors at Waldo Point were on the wrong side. If they wanted to advance their idea of using their property as they pleased, it would have been better for them to support Arques's wish to use his property as he pleased, by acknowledging his rights and paying him for the use of his property from the outset. As it was, Arques had no incentive to continue his fight with the county, so he just went along—in the event, to everyone's financial benefit.

Our country is loaded with opportunities, and they all flow from our hard won rights and freedoms, including the right to live as simply as possible and work as little as possible. It's called freedom of choice and in this country doesn't require riots or revolutions or getting angry or even feeling defensive. Only, perhaps, the exercising of a little discretion about where and how you do it since no one, except a politician trying to buy votes or a professional do-gooder looking for clients in order to justify a job, is particularly interested in supporting you if you are capable of supporting yourself.

So where were their parents and our educational system to explain all this to them in the first place? And how about the property owner? Lew Cook has to receive major credit for the survival of houseboats in the Waldo Point Harbor, including the protestor's boats. He had ample reason and justification to abandon the project he had bought into, turn the matter over to his attorneys, and go onto something less expensive and less combative. He didn't. He put his fortune, his reputation, and a good part of his future on the line for his investors and his inherited tenants. A lesser man would have folded.

After the extraordinary, long running start-up costs associated with this place, which of course the unsubsidized houseboaters mostly pay, whatever Lew gets he's earned and has every right to, just like each houseboat owner has every right to whatever they can get when they rent or sell. It's called incentive and reward for risking one's time, effort, and money on something one doesn't have to do. As a bonus, everyone at Waldo Point has benefited financially from Lew's efforts.

While there will always be the occasional dispute or disagreement between tenants and landlords, the house-boaters at Waldo Point have had way more in common with our landlord than with Big Brother. Indeed, whether everyone at Waldo is aware of it or not, we are deeply indebted to our landlord. Big Brother was usually absent when it counted, and when present was usually only looking out for its own skin and has mostly just been a major non-productive expense, which of course must be passed on to us, the end users. When speaking of government's contribution to the Waldo Point houseboat community, terms like negligence, abuse of discretion, unequal enforcement, political expediency, political cowardess, and huge costs come to mind.

The US Army Corps of Engineers, apparently taking a leaf from BCDC's book, is costing Lew Cook an open ended $700,000 in mitigation because of changes to accommodate the last thirty-eight boats whose owners refused berths under the original Corps permit, which didn't require any mitigation for the entire property! That's at least $18,400 per protester boat for just this instance of "mitigation," for boats the government itself promoted and is already subsidizing.

My, how they have learned to lever their power. It's as though nothing had happened at Waldo Point since 1969, that there wasn't a history, and that the Corps and BCDC hadn't been participants. It is true, the latest plan changes do call for covering up some pickleweed, but that pickleweed didn't exist until many years after our original permits were issued. We'd been stopped by illegal activity during which time the Corps and BCDC were conspicuously absent in the areas under their jurisdiction. Interesting and revealing exchanges of letters exist from those times that are not complimentary to either the Corps or the BCDC. For instance, BCDC took no action against either individual boat owners or the organization representing them who, under BCDC rules, brought unauthorized boats (considered bay fill) onto private and county property during the houseboat war. At the same time, BCDC demanded performance by the property owner in some of the areas occupied by those illegal boats while actually and specifically exempting those boats from its edicts, a "you can't get there from here" proposition for Lew Cook. If there is to be mitigation at Waldo Point it should run from government to the property owner and his original paying tenants. An apology and getting off Lew Cook's back would be nice.

* * *

Through it all, and despite everything, our neighborhood is indeed in a beautiful and unique place and is precious to those of us who live here, with our ever-changing sky and colors, and Mt. Tamalpais and the Strawberry peninsula, and the fog rolling over the ridges above Sausalito, and the water with its high and low tides and its birds and fish and mammals, and the prevailing northwest wind that cleans our air, and neighbors who look out for each other when storm winds blow. Our home.

With permission of the Marin Scope Newspapers, from the Week of February 6 – 12, 1973, Ed Long photographer. Picture probably dates from around 1959. Ferryboat *Charles Van Damm* is in the foreground, the ferryboat *Issaquah* is next, and behind it is the Spreckles House on a 110'x32'x9' wood barge. In the background, to the left of Spreckels, is the ferryboat *City of Seattle*.

Early 1960s. My dock, the tug *Leilani No. 3* and what was to become the Harbor office (8' x 8') from July 1969 until January 1977.

Ed Brady photo, March 4, 1969, from a slightly S.E. angle. Clipper Yacht Harbor is in the foreground, Waldo Point Harbor in the middle, and the horse-shoe shaped Kappas Lagoon in upper left. Gate 6 Road on the right (named by locals) runs up past Arques' block 227 and Mimi Tellis' harbor, with her *City of Seattle* at the outboard end. Kappas Harbor, then filled with house-boats, is at the end of Gate 6 Road.

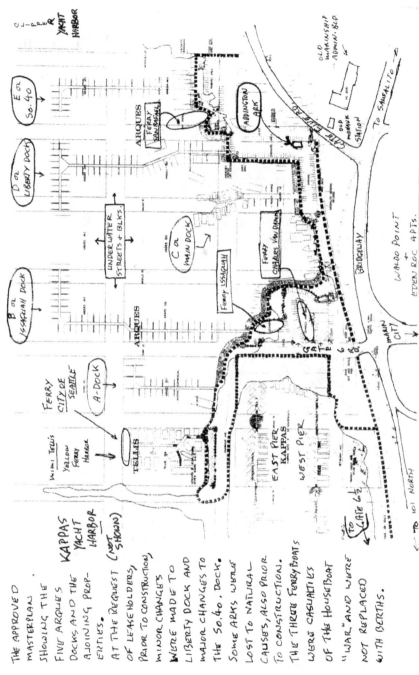

1975. Approved Masterplan.

After January 1, 1977. Shirley Flack in our new office on *Eight Brothers*, C.B. mike in one hand, phone under her ear, and ready to type.

Ed Brady Photo, February 9, 1977. Long view from the south. No visible work yet in Waldo Point Harbor. East and West Piers have been built in the Kappas Lagoon and occupied by houseboats from his old harbor where yachts are now berthed. Gate 6 ½ Pier, also named by locals, is just beyond East and West Piers. The Heliport houseboats can be seen in the distance just this side of the Richardson Bay Bridge. Across the Bay from the Houseboats is beautiful Strawberry Peninsula (looks best from the water). Note the dearth of houses in 1977.

September 11, 1977. Fred Peters (of "Fred's Place" fame), me, Vallerie of Jeff and Vallerie Harrison who own the ark *Benecia* on Main Dock, and an unidentified young man who is getting a lesson in how adults resolve their differences.

Chapter 15

What Now?

Over many years, I've concluded that we humans are inherently problem solvers, or at least try to be. It's probably a survival thing. I'm no different. So, while I wrestled with the drug problem at Waldo Point, I was constantly trying to understand it and figure out what could be done about it, not just try to get drugs out of our neighborhood.

Based on my observations and experience, including the use of self-help and remembering the lesson of Watergate, i.e., "follow the money," I came to some conclusions and possible courses of action.

My first conclusion was that those in the drug business are the same as any political demagogue who promises everything, but when you bite, delivers slavery. The promise of the drug business is to deliver an effortless shortcut to fun, bliss, nothingness, pleasure, or excitement, but what do you really get? When you finally realize it's all smoke and mirrors you often discover you are stuck with continuing payments on a contract that is very hard to break, and in many cases with consequences that cannot be reversed or repaired. Like the man said, no wonder it's called "dope"!

Perhaps you've come to something like the same conclusion and are pissed that your children or your friends or your neighborhood or your schools are targeted, and further, it's clear to you that standard "legal" solutions haven't and aren't correcting the problem. You feel you need to do something besides just complain to someone else.

First, look at the situation. We teach and lecture our children about how bad drugs are and about right and wrong, and then with a "good luck" and a pat on the back, we turn them lose to fight the dragons on their own. No wonder so many of them don't listen. They don't respect us when compared to drug dealers who thumb their nose at authority and have the guts to take risks, something that the young, who are straining against the leash of parental and school and societal control, can easily identify with, the old romanticized view of the highwayman and the pirate and the gangster.

When it comes to backing our words with deeds, we generally make poor role models. Mainly, I suspect, because we've been told for so long that government knows best and will take care of us and do everything for us, that we've come to believe it, even though history and experience and the cost, in all respects, tell us something quite different. What politician hasn't promised to do something for us, with our money, less government's cut and the ongoing cost of another bureaucracy, in exchange for votes?

Have we really forgotten how to take care of ourselves and look out for our own and each other? Or, to put it differently, have we become so enamored with authority that we automatically sit back and wait for someone else to stop something that we all know harms everyone? Isn't that the same as those who throughout history have excused what they did do by saying they were just following orders?

Faith that things will get better soon enough to have meaning in our lives has to have some basis, and I just don't see it the way things stand.

But how, you say, can you do anything about drugs or even find out what's going on when you have to work all day and are so tired when you come home at night, all you can do is flop down in your chair and catch up on Shakespeare? And besides, your kid is at school all day, and you don't even know most of your child's friends or what they do. Obviously, talk to your children, talk to their friends and to other parents and to your child's teachers.

In two days, if they don't already know, I could teach your eight year old how to recognize who is dealing and who is using in any suspect drug location where we are able to casually hang out and watch or surreptitiously observe. You can quickly figure it out yourself if you take some time out from work to watch and listen and ask questions and exchange information. An office building or business or factory or school or college might take longer. Now, you're thinking, if a child with so little training can recognize what's going on, why can't the cops? You're right, and they usually do know, but we'll explore that later.

And you're right about working and being tired. You have to pay taxes and rent or a mortgage, and you have to buy food and pay for medical insurance, etc., so your time is limited. The key is time management.

Presumably you have friends, other parents, relatives, and neighbors who feel as you do and would be willing to help if you approach them with a good case. You begin with one person and go on from there. Once you get help, you develop a plan and then split up the tasks, like guard duty.

Suppose, to make it simple, there is just one source of drugs on your street that is pretty obvious, and you want to shut it down. By far, your most valuable weapon is accurate intelligence. You don't want to go off half-cocked and accuse or hurt someone who is innocent or let the bad guys off the hook because you didn't do your homework. You arm yourselves with pen and paper and clocks and video cameras and still cameras and binoculars and tape recorders and make an accurate, detailed record of who, what, when and where, being careful to include dates, times, license numbers, and every possible detail related to your subject. You log everything, and be prepared to testify if necessary. It takes courage, right?

In this way, you will be able to document a pattern, identify the individuals involved, and be in a position to demand and get action from your local DA. Note: Before taking any direct action, always exhaust your administrative remedies and, most importantly, document your efforts. Best to approach the DA first because of their influence and the fact that they decide whether or not to prosecute once there's a bust. If you don't get a favorable response, you can put the system on the hot seat while you go to plan B.

Having documented the problem and failing to get "legal" help, I would first simply go talk to the people involved, one at a time if there is more than one drug store you want to close, and politely explain your position and ask them to move. If that doesn't work, and of course you can't trust what they tell you, or if you just get lip or threats in return, there are a number of things you can do. Burning down the building might not be the best idea as some innocent might get hurt or the fire might damage someone else's house or building, and firemen are always at risk. Instead, finding out who owns the building and starting a nuisance action for money damages can be very effective because if you win your case the damages continue until the nuisance is removed. Coupled with a rent strike, this is particularly useful in an apartment building. A nuisance action will also reflect badly on the DA, which is only fair.

A nuisance action by an adjacent property owner about activity on one of Arques's other properties was the only thing I ever saw that made him jump. All his attorneys told him the same thing—get rid of the subject of the suit, fast. And he did. A nuisance action requires a good attorney, which may or may not be possible in your situation, and an action in law may take longer than you are willing to wait. In either case you may have to proceed on your own.

Unless there is violence associated with your drug scene, staging a daylight hex might work. That is, set up an obvious "picket" in front. Visibly take pictures, maybe hold signs, write down license numbers, etc. In other words make your point publicly, but peacefully, until you disrupt their ability to do business to the extent they are forced to move. One should not try to do this alone. Also, tell the police what you are going to do and ask for a patrol car or two to park in front because of "the possibility of violence." Be sure to log your requests for assistance. If headquarters doesn't cooperate, ask an individual patrolman for help or call in a disturbance or call the dogcatcher saying there is a mad dog loose or shots fired, anything to rattle everyone's cage and get action. Don't call in a fire alarm because that may deny help to someone who really needs it. And, make sure before you start that you get to know and become friendly with the local police. You want them on your side.

A TV station might be attracted to do a story on your efforts, but beware; when they go home you may still have the problem, without the fanfare, and the media may also use your actions as a basis for a series on the dangers of citizens taking the law into their own hands— stock formula to keep a story controversial and alive—and you may find the cops hustling you away instead of the dealers. The media's interests and objectives are not necessarily the same as yours despite what they may say to you in order to get a quote, and they won't be there to help when the fecal matter hits the fan. If you want publicity, I suggest you find a print journalist who is dedicated to truth and accuracy, read their work, and cultivate that person for some serious, long-term, in-depth journalism. That is one of the most effective paths to true reform of the system you are laboring under, providing you keep up the pressure.

Once you've started, if you find yourselves subject to a legal action for harassment, or whatever, you have your documentation to back your play, including your efforts to get "legal" help. Demand a jury trial and get your information into the record and make it as public as possible. If your activity has been both necessary and has been conducted with honor, there is a good chance one or more jurors will hang it, even if you are guilty as hell of whatever you are accused of. Among other things in your favor, the jurors will probably dislike the lawyers representing the dopers if it's a civil case or the DA if it's a criminal case against you.

So the dealers persist, and you're not making headway, and maybe your helpers are getting tired of the extra duty and are fearful of retaliation. The opposite can also occur. Conflict can draw neighbors closer together and stiffen their resolve. In either case, it's time for covert action.

* * *

Vehicles, including customers' cars, phone lines, electric lines and meters, gas lines and meters, water lines and meters, TV cables, sewer lines (maybe via clean-outs), and garbage cans and debris boxes are all illegal and effective targets. Like a siege of old, you deny the entrenched the things they need for day-to-day operation, but expect counter measures and increased guard duty requirements. Best and most effective if you can hit a lot of items at once. It makes a bigger and maybe impossible problem for them to correct, makes your side appear to be very strong and well organized, and weakens their opportunities for and interest in retaliation. Always have backups and if at all possible, a friendly cop(s) nearby to help neutralize reactions.

Try finding out if anyone insures the building where the drug action is taking place or if there are loans on it, and alert them to what's going on and the potential for losses if the dealing continues. In other words, you have to throw away the rulebook, rely on yourselves, be innovative, expect casualties—better you than your children—and most of all, stick with it until you succeed. If you fail, you might as well turn over your homes to them and move. At some point, if you persist, politicians will start to pay attention because the squeaky wheel does get the grease. Your children will also start seeing you with different eyes.

If you live in subsidized housing or if your problem location is an abandoned building(s) your options actually improve. You need the usual solid intelligence, then, in the first case; you simply get together with your neighbors and go on a well-publicized rent strike against the government entity that administers your housing. The basis is that your landlord is denying you the quiet enjoyment of your leasehold by allowing nuisances to exist. It doesn't require all of you to do it, but the more the better, and make sure you get continuous publicity until the problem is solved. Also, there are rules that go with rent strikes, so make sure you talk to an attorney during the planning stage. If you do it by the book, it announces to the judge that you are serious people, not just trying to avoid paying rent.

In other words, your landlord, the government, or their agent has not responded to your complaints and is thereby permitting drug dealing, which is a nuisance by any standard, and you want them to stop permitting it. It's a civil action, so if it goes to court you don't need the same level of proof as in a criminal case. I guarantee you will make your government/landlord jump. The media will love it, unless they are in bed with the local politicians, because it amounts to a scandal, and they can target politicians and bureaucrats and the use and misuse of tax money. Make sure, also, that preventative measures are in place before you resume paying rent or the situation will revert once the heat's off since negligent management caused the problem in the first place.

In the case of abandoned buildings, ask local government to correct the problem and if they don't, sue them for negligence, permitting nuisances to exist, etc., and seek a writ of mandate to compel them to act—all juicy stuff for the media and for the political party out-of-power. In both cases, all other options are available, but try going after government first, less dangerous.

If people you know are involved in the drug scene and you are worried about a "code of silence," don't be. Be up front with them. Whether or not they like it, they'll respect you for it. They are the ones who are hurting others and if they have any brains left they know it. Besides, it's a wake up call and ten to one, if they pay attention, you'll be saving them from a bigger fall later with more severe consequences.

* * *

What about schools, you say? It is a simple fact that most young people are introduced to illegal drugs by other students, often their friends and acquaintances, just like with alcohol and cigarettes.

The growing popularity of private schools versus public schools—also note the growth of home schooling—is indicated by the waiting lists and the stiff competition for admission to most of them. Two of the underlying reasons are drugs and the dumbing down of many public schools, often attributable to or exacerbated by drugs and related behavior problems. Drugs are not absent in even the best private schools, but, intervention and help are more readily available, and there's not the same dollar-based reluctance to expel problem students that exists in much of the public school system.

If we messed around when I was young, some adult was usually paying attention, and we suffered immediate consequences, so bad behavior was often checked before it went to the next level. Nowadays it's much different, is often related to drugs, and as a result, we are offering the criminal system in this country a constant stream of qualified apprentices. Not good.

Speaking of consequences, when I was seven to nine, doing my two years in a military school, the guy in charge had a wide leather belt, a ping-pong paddle, and a board with holes in the business end and a handle at the other end. He was fair though. He laid down the law and always did what he said he'd do. Believe me, we paid attention, and it was the rare kid indeed who got paddled more than once. I seem to recall I was one of those. I've also got to say that most of us loved the guy. His name was Bill McCafferty. He taught us, he trained us, and on Sunday nights when we came back from visits with our parents—those who were able to—he read to us. He knew it helped take our minds off the separation.

The two sides of the coin are: You can't keep a student around who is hurting or endangering others and yet you also do what you can to get them back into the fold (but without risk to others). Simply transferring a problem student to another school doesn't eliminate the problem or help the student. It does, though, keep money coming into the school district if school funding is based on body count, which is absolutely the wrong incentive for the system. In short, we either permit drugs in our schools or we don't. There is no in between.

The bottom line is protecting your children and their futures, not protecting the school or teachers' jobs.

One must judge government and all other forms of vested interests by their actions, not their words. Forming committees to study a problem is not an action. Also, and this is a biggie, do not accept the excuse that schools don't have enough money to set high standards. If a school or a school system or teachers don't set and demand high standards of behavior and performance and help the students achieve those standards to the highest extent of each child's gifts, they aren't earning the money they already get. Money is not the objective anyway, or shouldn't be. Education is the objective. The difference is in attitude and commitment. Then they are worth gold.

I would add here a last thought on schools in the form of a quote from the economist Walter E. Williams who stated, in part, in his presentation, "The Poor as First Victims of the Welfare State," in 1980 at Hillsdale College, Hillsdale, Michigan "As empirical evidence. . . albeit anecdotal, is the readily made observation of any city slum. The observer would see some nice cars, some nice homes, some nice clothes and some nice food, but no nice schools. Such an observation would be puzzling were it not for an appreciation of how cars, houses, clothes and food are distributed versus how schools are distributed. The former are distributed, for the most part, by the market mechanism, while schools are distributed by the political mechanism. It turns out, incidentally, that there are a few nice schools in some slums. And interestingly enough these schools, for the most part, are produced outside the state education monopoly; they are the parochial schools, private community schools and Black Muslim schools."

Black parents in our nation's capital apparently agree and have been fighting for years to get a permanent, reliable voucher system in place so they can have the choice of where to send their children to school.

One other "Watch out!" and that is: If you get a movement going to remove drugs from your neighborhood or your school, don't let yourselves be co-opted by groups or individuals with other political agendas. Keep your objective narrow and focused and pure, at least until you are successful. Otherwise you will dilute your support, lose sympathy, and inherit your new "ally's" opposition.

* * *

How about the police? In the final analysis, our rule of law, that is, the will-of-the-people as expressed through laws passed by our representatives, comes from the presence of a night stick or a gun in the hands of the men and women we hire to do our dirty work. Most police officers I've met are honest, gutsy, and dedicated. We tie their hands with rules and regulations and set high standards because history has correctly taught us to fear the potential for abuse by all people in power. It's a tricky balance, but works well in this country because as citizens, we are generally informed, have most of our eyes open, and because we all share the same fundamental values. The continuing existence of the drug trade is not the fault of the guys on the beat or in the patrol car, but more in the priorities and the will of our political leaders, those who decide policy—that is, who gets charged, who goes to trial, how resources are allocated and, most importantly, what the law says.

Unconventional wars have taught us that if you don't secure the hamlets, you can't win the war. Picture the kid in school who "acts out" and interrupts the class. If he is just shushed and allowed to get away with it, the rest of the class suffers because the lesson doesn't get taught or absorbed as well, and the problem child is encouraged to continue his antics because the system has shown fear or indifference, and there has been no consequence for bad behavior. The child is also apt to realize, correctly, that nobody cares enough about him to be honest with him, correct his behavior, and urge him along a different path—the view from the bottom is quite clear—and that kind of realization certainly does not inspire constructive feelings. The lowest common denominator then rules.

That is what happens when drug action on the streets is ignored or tolerated while the major resources are directed at the "big guys," the big newsworthy cases. Don't stop going after big guys, but also make sure there is no one available to sell their products on the street at the other end.

There is, however, a big, major, overriding, deal killer catch in all this, and it is where "follow the money" comes into it. As long as drug users are treated with kid gloves, as long as there is no serious legal, and more importantly, financial consequence to using drugs, the demand will continue and there will always be young men and women who are willing to risk prison for the "easy money" derived from drug sales; the trade will continue to flourish.

Drug users finance the drug trade, i.e., abet a mammoth, if disjointed, criminal enterprise, not to mention causing or contributing to the destabilization of entire countries such as our immediate neighbor to the south-there is no other way to describe it-and there are two obvious solutions. We either legalize drugs, saying that drug use is alright, and then flood the market with cheap drugs, and in the process, abandon a percentage of our population, including our youth, to addiction and worse, and as a society suffer all the predictable side effects, or, we start going after the users as well as the dealers, providing mandatory—custodial if necessary—treatment for those who are out of control and making it so expensive for the rest that it is no longer smart, cool, fun, or affordable to mess with drugs.

As long as the user door is open, all the rest of it is just a big, expensive make work project. Such a change in policy would no doubt be a political hot potato, but in my opinion, it is necessary. If well-healed users were fined, say 10% of their adjusted gross income and double for each additional bust, the war on drugs and treatment of addicts could be self-financing. I suspect that the entertainment industry would be well represented on the contribution side.

Because the people who buy illegal drugs provide the incentive for drug dealers, it's only logical that they pay the costs associated with solving the problem. And think of the leverage we'd gain to get information and testimony from both sides of the equation.

If the demand for drugs shrinks, the price of drugs will drop as dealers compete for buyers. The profits that justified the risk will shrink, young men might become disillusioned with the business, and even our crowded prisons might get a break. Walter E. Williams would say, "Such a prediction is consistent with a wide body of economic theory which predicts that as the cost of an action (or good) rises, people will do less of it." We should try everything, keeping in mind that youth goes fast, and the clock is always ticking for our sons and daughters.

Right now there is a lot of indifference to the subject of drugs and their victims. Probably because the primary victims tend to become invisible since they usually drop out of the mainstream. Then, if they are thought of at all it is only as losers, or poor him or poor her, and then they are forgotten, much as we've grown accustomed to seeing and thinking of and forgetting about down-and-out alcoholics.

Unless they are part of your family, then they are a tragedy. The person who is strung out doesn't have an easy choice in the matter, that's why it's called an addiction. On the other hand, the "for personal use only" recreational user does have an easy choice. They are the high end of the trade, and with a few busts here and few busts there, a few busts everywhere, on a continuous basis with mandatory stiff fines; it won't be long before word gets out that drugs are no longer cool, no longer smart, and most importantly, no longer affordable. I know people who won't go to a party anymore where alcohol is served except by cab or with a reliable designated driver because to them it has become just too expensive and time consuming to risk a DUI. If we make that kind of risk true for drug use, in a really serious way, we can cripple the trade and significantly reduce the danger to our children and to our society and to our neighbors to the south.

Unfortunately, it is painfully obvious that the requirement for success in all of this is for individual citizens to kick-start the process by taking charge of the solution ourselves, one way or another, beginning where we live. Who knows better than we do what goes on in our own apartment buildings, our own neighborhoods, and our own cities? Back in the late '60s, before I got involved with harbor problems, I had a friend who worked at Fred's restaurant in Sausalito and lived with her boyfriend in a quiet '50s neighborhood behind the Cove Shopping Center in Tiburon. A great Italian restaurant there, by the way, called Milano's. Anyway, the occupants of the house across the street from them were dealing drugs, and there was a lot of obvious traffic. Some of the neighbors didn't like that very much, so they made a record of cars, license numbers, and dates and times, which was sufficient to establish a pattern that the local police department was able to follow-up on. The place got raided and closed down. I think she said that the whole process only took three or four weeks. It's possible to be effective if we act.

If we don't step forward and confront the drug problem, the sale and use of drugs will doubtlessly continue as usual, and one day we will see politicians seeking the dope vote because by default, illegal drugs, like tobacco and alcohol, will become an accepted part of our culture and traffickers and dealers and users will become special interest groups whose approval and votes and, especially money, will be sought by those trying to gain or hold onto political power. Or, we will see people in government promoting legalization and control of drugs so they can feed their vote buying spending habits with the profits, instead of jeopardizing their political futures by continuously raising taxes, for a while at least, just as they did with gambling, which by comparison is harmless.

Our lawmakers and our police and our criminal justice system have not stopped the drug trade. Individual citizens working together can upset that status quo and like Mothers Against Drunk Drivers (MADD), we can change the landscape and attitudes and public opinion. One drug store and one drug dealer (and one hung jury?) at a time if necessary.

"What about the rights of the accused, the presumption of innocence?" you say. When anyone's rights are put at risk, the standard response is that we are all put at risk. That is universally accepted as true in this country with our values and under our system of law. I believe that, too. However, there is an ugly aspect to this; the victims of crime often pay the price for preserving our rights. So, do we let victims continue to protect our rights and accept it as a necessary price, or do we say "screw it," get justice for the victims, and take the chance of becoming defendants ourselves? Sometimes yes? Sometimes no? It's never been an easy question. When our children are at risk, the answer to me is a no brainer—whatever the personal cost.

* * *

Where does the 4th Estate come into this? I've heard it said that the best thing about our free press, including most forms of public information sources—C-Span being one of the noteworthy exceptions—is that it's not an un-free press. Well no one expects human perfection because that wouldn't be human, and anyway, perfection in human affairs usually means a narrow set of attitudes and rules dictated by a self-styled elite (that is definitely contrary to the American concept of free speech). It is, after all, our freedom to disagree and debate and to publicly test ideas and to make fools of ourselves that makes us strong, proud, and open to endless possibilities in all areas of life; it is free speech that defines democracy.

The people who report the "news" and those who own the businesses that pay them and pay their taxes and pay their stock holders, etc., are in large measure the source we all turn to for information from outside our immediate lives, and the different elements and parts of the media constantly compete for our attention. They have to in order to stay in businesses. We are their customers, and they often pander to our perceived tastes and color information with current fads and fashions and use gimmicks as a means of getting and holding our attention. Being human, they also tend to spin or interpret the news to reflect their political biases or to maintain "sources," and they also favor the attention getting, the controversial, and the sensational in order to increase market share or ratings, which attracts the advertisers who pay the bills and insure their salaries. Perfectly all right. It's a direct expression of free speech and economic freedom, and while that style of reporting is perhaps not the purest form of journalism, it is superior to any form of control or censorship from on high.

It's also where "if it bleeds, it leads" comes from. Charles McCabe, quoted posthumously in a May 5th 1983 column in the *San Francisco Chronicle*, wrote, "When I was breaking in as a reporter on a Hearst newspaper in New York City, I once submitted a tale full of Christian charity and the milk of human kindness. As I recall, it was about a kid who brought hot food to a Bowery bum every day. It was all heart, that story.

"The city editor read it, motioned to me and took me aside. He said, 'Nice story, Charlie. I'll take it home and read it to my kids. But it won't make the paper. Around here, bad news is good news, and don't you forget it.'"

That can have profound effects on the rest of us, though, with our innocent propensity to believe what we hear or read the first time around, particularly if it is something sensational or negative or fits our preconceived ideas, which is why political attack ads are so successful. As often happens, the press and politicians will cynically adopt such attention-getting stories or causes to run with. One of the most damaging examples of that was the pseudo-scientific theory of Eugenics, also known as Racial Hygiene or Social Darwinism, which was popular early in the last century up to the point Hitler adopted it as part of his racial-superiority-thing before World War II. He sold it to the German people at a cost of some 70,000 German lives. The German people themselves finally called a halt to most of it when they realized that dear old *grossvater und mutter* had been included in the program.

After World War II and Hitler's other activities in Europe became common knowledge, the Western World, including our own politicians, academics, and the press, dropped eugenics like a hot potato. For a quick review of eugenics read the back section of Michael Crichton's *State of Fear*. Or, for a source book, written by "experts," read *The Science of Eugenics and Sex-Life, Love, Marriage, Maternity: The Regeneration of the Human Race* by Walter J. Hadden, MD, Fellow Royal College of Surgeons, Charles H. Robinson, biologist, and Mary Ries Melendy, MD, PhD, and edited by Robert L. Leslie, MD, copyright 1904 by W. R. Vansant.

Today's popular "crisis" is global warming, or as it is now being called, climate change, which so many in and out of government have bought into on the basis of what appears to me to be more of an exercise in applied political science than physical science. Wasn't it an ice age we were being warned about in the '70s? It's alright though. While the cost can be high as we wait for the truth to struggle out, the alternative to free speech is no freedom. For another perspective on global warming read *Unstoppable Global Warming: Every 1,500 Years* by S. Fred Singer and Dennis T. Avery.

I say our system and the free speech it represents is healthy and dynamic, and woe be to him who tries to tinker with any part of it. I include here two of my favorite attributed quotes on the subject of censorship from notes by A. Ranney Johnson, economist and historian: "I shall never tolerate the newspapers to say or do anything against my interests; they may publish a few little articles with just a little poison in them, but one fine morning somebody will shut their mouths" (Napoleon Bonaparte), and sometime later, "Why should freedom of speech and freedom of the press be allowed? Why should a government which is doing what it believes to be right allow itself to be criticized? It would not allow opposition by lethal weapons. Ideas are much more fatal things than guns. Why should any man be allowed to buy a printing press and disseminate pernicious opinions calculated to embarrass the government" (Vladimir Ilyich Lenin).

Our task is to check the information that's being thrown at us, or at least not take it too seriously, since we may have no personal experience or understanding at the moment by which to evaluate either the particular information or, as importantly, the source. Just because something is in print or is spoken by a sincere sounding talking head or by a politician or a supposed expert, does not guarantee that the information presented is accurate or complete, or in context, or even relevant. Personally, if events didn't move so fast, I would generally prefer to wait for the books.

Information from the media isn't a one-way process. Citizens can be heard too. For instance, deaths in auto accidents are often reported, sometimes with pictures. Why aren't overdoses reported? The people are just as dead, but of course there is no wreckage or blood to be seen, and death by drugs doesn't make good copy unless it's a celebrity, then story is about the celebrity, not the drugs. If we as customers of the media want more attention paid to the subject of illegal drugs, we can push to get it or we can promote a story of why we aren't getting it. Don't assume good will on the part of the media and also remember that your story is in competition with other stories.

One beef with the media, given their immense power to influence, is that so little of their effort goes into continuous hard looks at the damage done to our youth and their education and to the people who have had to live without protection from that infestation, sometimes for generations, because it has been treated like a given in certain areas rather than as a dangerous cancer that drags down people's lives.

Obviously the death of some junkie isn't going to be able to compete with a starlet's latest adventures just because that dead junkie was once a baby and the light of someone's life, but I think that the very power and influence of the press creates an obligation to report that premature death and its significance.

* * *

As for houseboats, the most revealing of all of our coverage were the articles about our last BCDC hearing when the commission gave their final approval to our last plan on March 18, 2004. Those few articles were lightweight feel good stories quoting the "usual sources." So, what's the big deal? Well, I grew up with the notion that the obligation of a free press, along with making a successful business, and this has been said many times, is to report facts and to ask hard questions, to inform, to focus the spotlight, and, most crucially, to constantly question and challenge those in power, to be our skeptical watch dog, so as a free people we can be better armed to protect our freedoms. That's not too much to ask to go along with the ads and the entertainment and the political slants. Our last BCDC hearing was an opportunity for someone in the local press to ask or review some of the open questions about our little affair. How did it all start? What were the issues? What happened?

And, what did government do relative to those issues and those events, and why did it all take so damn long?

And by the way, what did it end up costing, in all respects? Without seeing the numbers, it is my guess that the property owner has spent as much money since 1977 on security, attorneys, and the incredibly long running planning process for Waldo Point as on the purchase of the property itself and the construction of the first five docks and related facilities.

In comparison to the amount of time we spent in "planning," it's instructive to recall what was accomplished just next door to us during the World War II years.

On March 2, 1942, a telegram was received by the W. A. Bechtel Company from the chairman of the United States Maritime Commission asking them to build and operate a new shipyard on the West Coast. The company agreed to do so that same day. A tentative building site was proposed in Sausalito, the city consulted with a positive response, and the next day, March 3, the Maritime Commission was advised of and approved the site selection. On March 9, six days later, an estimate of $9,300,000 for a six-way yard was submitted in Washington and after a ten-minute discussion regarding a further requirement to be able to later convert for tankers, the estimate was raised to $10,250,000. On March 12, 1942, a contract was awarded on a cost-plus, two-dollars fee basis. On March 18, a press conference was held, and thereafter, care was taken to maintain sound relations with Marin and surrounding counties. Condemnation legal procedures took about two weeks, and construction of the shipyard started on March 28,1942—twenty-six days after the initiating telegram from the Maritime Commission. Three months later, on June 27, the first keel was laid. By the end of 1942, six months later, seven ships had been launched and five delivered. Elapsed time: nine months and twenty-nine days.

Granted, those were emergency times and the Bechtel Co. and their associates had ongoing experience in what they were being asked to do, there were no mysteries to overcome. In 1969, there were no mysteries for what we were trying to do, either, and what we proposed was infinitely simpler in terms of both planning and execution than what had been accomplished next door in Marinship. There was nothing at Waldo Point that a person with a modicum of experience and background on the waterfront, me for instance, couldn't plan conceptually in a few hours and then build in a reasonable time—absent roadblocks. Were there any monumental issues that required forty-two years of government talk to resolve? No.

In contrast to Marinship during World War II, a very clear comparison of how our modern government functions is found in a March 16, 2008 *Independent Journal* article by Dick Spotswood regarding a wheel chair ramp. He wrote, in part:

"The Bay Area is witnessing a classic contrast between the way affairs are managed in some big American cities and how they can be accomplished in the suburban private sector.

"Some large institutions, both public and private, have tendencies to act in a manner in which proposed solutions to basic problems become so complicated and expensive that little is ever accomplished. Others by leadership and necessity manage to foster an institutional culture where the search for the simplest remedy at the lowest cost is the norm.

"That dichotomy popped up regarding a flap over the San Francisco Board of Supervisors' historic chamber. That room is equipped with a podium from which the board's president presides. It is not accessible to the physically disabled. Supervisor Michela Alioto-Pier, who is partially paralyzed and uses a wheelchair, has reasonably asked for a ramp to reach the dais. After a year going through the city's Byzantine bureaucracy, city supervisors were presented with a $1.1 million plan to build the wheelchair ramp.

"The supervisors, understandably stupefied by the estimate, were then told that perhaps a few pennies could be shaved off the project, but it's inevitably a seven-figure job. City supervisors ended up rejecting the plan and Alioto-Pier promised litigation.

"Mill Valley's O'Hanlon Center for the Arts recently found that its art gallery was not accessible and a wheelchair ramp was needed. With a Mill Valley Rotary grant, in less than a week, they built a new portable ramp somewhat longer than the 10-foot ramp proposed for San Francisco's Board of Supervisors' chamber. The cost: $1,200.

"San Francisco has a public sector culture dependent upon hordes of consultants and large staff. *With zero physical work accomplished on the wheelchair ramp, they have managed to rack up $232,000 in design costs, consultant bills and permit fees.*

"The O'Hanlon Center followed a different approach. It just called in a handyman and the work was done in a few days. Yes, O'Hanlon is a private institution, but the task was the same. The contrast is a lesson for all large institutions on both sides of the bay that common sense and a can-do attitude doesn't have to be a foreign concept in the public sector."

* * *

The most significance aspect and lesson of our story, from my perspective, is not the soon-forgotten houseboats, or the drugs, or even the people, God love us, but rather how our government, at all levels, conducts itself and especially the reasons for its conduct. Those questions deserve our attention because the answers reveal how our government, the people in whom we've granted power over us, actually operate and how they have grown to view themselves and their jobs and in what low esteem they must hold the rest of us.

Our experience at Waldo Point suggests that once elected or hired, the focus of most people in government is to hang onto their jobs and their power, which includes a *carte blanche* to think up work for themselves, as well as an assumed right to keep their heads down in anything that doesn't earn them promotions or votes or that might cause them problems. There doesn't seem to be a standard of right and wrong or an acceptance of responsibility by most of our paid decision makers, only self-serving expediency.

In our case, by ducking responsibility, government left the hard stuff in the residents' laps three times over a very long period of time. First, we had to deal with the heroin problem ourselves, then it was guarding our new docks so they could get and stay built, then there were the additional years of diminished quiet enjoyment, and the attendant costs, while we waited for the other shoe to drop.

Someone who runs a business like government operates would get fired, unless of course he can afford to make campaign contributions to the right politicians, who will then defend his practices and bail him out with our tax money when everything collapses in a heap. Like the key senators and representatives in Washington D.C. who reportedly received large campaign contributions from the executives of Fannie and Freddie while blocking reforms to those institutions that were to contribute so much to our 2008 financial meltdown.

Other than backing the people running against them, there's probably not much we can do about entrenched senators and representatives from other states. They are smart enough to bring home the bacon in order to ingratiate themselves with their contributors and their constituencies. That's always been the game, and as a nation we make that possible because for many of us, without looking too hard, a bird in the hand, however anemic, is often seen as preferable to the more difficult and sometimes hard to know but superior course of action. Short-term benefits are easy to offer and easier to accept and tend to put us to sleep, but are rarely the best for us.

We are a nation of overlapping special interests—political and economic diversity—a good thing. However, too much focus by us on our own special interests makes it easy to forget the principals in the Constitution that are the foundation of our freedoms and our resulting prosperity. Shortsighted self-interest erodes those principals and with them our freedoms, and when freedom goes prosperity goes. There is always a politician available on a street corner eager to sell his or her vote to the highest bidder in exchange for campaign contributions, party backing, or support from special interest groups, in order to enhance or stay in power, always at the expense of other citizens. The street corner politician's only concern is where his or her interest lies at that moment and which taxes to raise or who's freedoms to diminish in order to provide their John with the purchased inside tract.

A dangerous side effect of our competition to get the best deal from those we elect is that we frequently end up giving more power to government, thus diminishing our own power over and responsibility for our own lives, what we know as liberty. It's a Ponzi scheme where ultimately the only winners are those in government. When we cede power to government in exchange for special deals to improve or protect our special interests, we implicitly grant government the power to take away as well as bestow. The danger is, one day we will wake up and discover we have no choices anymore—government will control everything. And we all know how efficient and just and capable government is. Do you personally know any man or woman or group of people to whom you would entrust that much power over your life? I didn't think so. So what makes us think that power-obsessed human beings in Washington D.C. or our state capitols or in our entrenched bureaucracies, are better than us? Because they and their partners in the media say so?

The only way to change our vote selling and vote buying political culture is for the rest of us to pay closer attention to what's going on and demand a high standard of conduct from the people we elect to represent us. If they fail, vote them out of office again and again until they get the message. If we fail, it will be like Madison Avenue's favorite, current buzzword: We will "deserve" what we get. That's it in a nutshell. We either pay attention or get screwed.

All of us have skin in the game. In other words, we all have something to lose. I know it doesn't always seem that way, which is probably why so many of us don't bother to pay attention, and as result politician's find us so easy to lead by the nose. In fact, the extent to which we inform ourselves not only shapes our future, but likely our children's and their children, even when it's not immediately obvious how or why. In the best of worlds, an informed electorate would greatly reduce the effectiveness of big money contributions, the attack ads they finance, and the resulting ease with which politicians manipulate us. We could force ideas and policy to be the focus in elections, with each candidate having to explain to us in detail why their ideas and their policies would be best for our country. Politicians would become accountable in the process, political soap operas would be sent back to daytime TV, and the 4ᵗʰ Estate would be forced to resume its role as watchdog in order to stay ahead of us.

Like the man said, freedom is not free.

Thomas Jefferson said, "The natural order of things is for liberty to yield and government gain ground." Friedrich Hayek referred to it as *The Road to Serfdom*, and Benjamin Franklin concluded, "They that can give up essential liberty to obtain a little temporary safety deserve neither liberty nor safety." Mark Twain added, "It could probably be shown by facts and figures that there is no distinctly Native American criminal class except Congress." Mark Twain was a very funny guy, but he rarely joked.

Politicians using special favors and handouts to buy votes or support is a constant in the world of politics and works just fine up to the last guys in office who face riots and expulsions when the payoffs can no longer be supported by revenues in a ruined economy. Gifts of money or special deals, either to buy votes or intended as an acts of compassion to help someone get back on their feet, frequently become obligations or permanent entitlements in the eyes of the recipients, as well as in the eyes of those whose jobs depend on handing out the money or administering the favors, another constant in the world of politics long familiar to Europeans. Government guarantees and "too big to fail" fall into that category, and both have negative side effects and serious long-term consequences. We've missed the bullet so far, but are being pushed hard in that direction by the "Big Brother knows best" crowd.

A particularly disturbing aspect of all this is that those who work for government and are direct beneficiaries of more and bigger government have become a single-interest voting block in this country with a dramatically disproportionate influence on public policy by becoming treasuries for those seeking elective office. They have become lobbies for their own form of growth industry. Of course they have that right as individuals, as well as the right to act collectively for those who choose to, but what about politicians who become obligated to those special interests? Don't the people we elect have a duty to serve a much broader constituency? Since politics is largely the art of acquiring and keeping power, is it unreasonable to conclude that money buys loyalty? Do we really want to vote for someone who is on retainer to represent one group ahead of all others, regardless of what he or she may say in order to get elected? Follow the money.

A tough part about actually governing is that you will almost never make everyone happy at the same time, and you always run the risk of alienating powerful special interests that may turn on you and support your opponent. However, an honest job does demand that you decide and act on what you think is best for the country, despite the political risks. Being a good leader not only requires honesty and judgment but also courage.

Like the hierarchy of any established power structure—businesses, unions, churches, colleges, etc.—those in charge in government are institutionally conditioned to constantly seek additional areas of authority and funding. It's called empire-building, a survival and advancement necessity, usually with little regard to the long-range effect on the rest of us. Unlike other institutions, those in government are able to impose their expansion with the force of law. Businesses are the most self-correcting because they must constantly compete and actually produce something and because of the scrutiny they receive from the market place, boards-of-directors, and stockholders.

An inherent problem with government, unlike the "private sector," is that it is not subject to competition as we know it and is therefore often freed from the consequences of its actions, except for every two, four, or six years, and even then our short attention span and intervening events often let them off the hook. A large part of what has made it all work, so far, are challenges from the opposition, others seeking political power, and our free press—part of the genius of our Constitution. Competition inside government, on the other hand, for our tax money, is intense. Picture a big pot of juicy scraps that taxpayers are compelled to provide and a pack of hungry dogs. There is never enough. Government by its nature is power hungry and constantly needs more money to feed its ambitions. And we, wittingly or unwittingly, have been the enablers, so long as we get our special deals or are too disinterested to pay attention.

* * *

As to the media, other than some noted exceptions, the important questions about our Waldo Point experience were not asked during the conflict, during the extended planning phase, or at the last symbolic plan approval by the BCDC when the best the press could offer was a saccharin "Ho-hum."

The final BCDC plan approval hearing was held almost thirty-five years after I started the process in 1969. At forty-two years and counting, Lew Cook still does not have the actual building permits required to complete the work.

Not interesting? Not newsworthy? Boring? I agree, and that is the point.

The combination of the sleep inducing dullness and the blindingly thick complexity of government procedure which passes for governing these days is the smoke behind which government has been able to steadily grow over the years and is the means for increasingly gratuitous and excessive regulation and its companion taxation that perpetuates the system and along with it, government careers. Entire industries of attorneys, accountants, advisors, and consultants have been grown to interpret the mess for us, who in turn have become vested in the system, as we are ever further distanced from those we elect, who are supposed to represent us, not the system.

In defense of government, Charles Dickens probably pleads their case best in a quote from his book *Bleak House*, first published in 1852 and 1853 as a serial, when he states, "The one great principle of the English law is to make business for itself. There is no other principle distinctly, certainly, and consistently maintained through all its narrow turnings. Viewed by this light it becomes a coherent scheme and not the monstrous maze the laity are apt to think it. Let them but once clearly perceive that its grand principle is to make business for itself at their expense, and surely they will cease to grumble."

Shame on us for being so gullible and self absorbed and shame on the press for not doing a better job.

How about a national referendum to abolish all federal and state withholding taxes. If the citizens who pay taxes have to voluntarily take a chunk of the money they earn each week back out of their pockets and send it to government, they are probably going to sit up straight and say, "Whoa! Where is this money going?" Wouldn't it be nice if every dollar that politicians spend had to be justified to us instead of just to each other in exchange for reciprocated favors? Sure, it would be awkward and cumbersome, but wouldn't it be fun to watch them scramble.

As to forty-two years in the planning process, I have no doubt that if our little houseboat affair had been kept solely in Marin County's jurisdiction it would have been resolved in the '70s, everyone in berths by 1980, and the three historic ferryboats would still exist. It would have worked because we would have only been dealing with an accessible local government responsive to an electorate and accountable under law instead of distant, insulated, super agencies staffed and run by un-elected and un-accountable professional bureaucrats who march to who knows what drummers or what special interests or what pressure groups. Bureaucracies like the BCDC don't understand or try to understand the citizens they dictate to, but only follow whatever cause (and backers) they've adopted regardless of the cost or benefits to those affected by their actions. Local governments have always been the best agents to act as servants of the people because local governments are visible to and have to live with the people they govern and their actions also tend to be more cost effective.

Our San Francisco Bay Conservation and Development Commission, the BCDC, and the building moratorium that proceeded its enabling authority, were necessary and good ideas at the outset because they addressed real concerns about the filling and the future of San Francisco Bay. But enough time has elapsed now, enough information has been collected, enough experience has been gained, enough guidelines have been drawn, enough principles have been generally accepted, and enough precedents have been established so that local jurisdictions can handle the same permit applications without being babysat by a regional agency with its endless duplication of effort and the associated costs to applicants, taxpayers, and consumers.

In other words, like the attorney who has won his case, the BCDC has done its job and is now just milking the clock. Bureaucracies, like wars, are difficult to control once started. Bureaucracies tend to take on a life of their own; their primary objective is to insure their longevity by holding onto and increasing their power.

Back on January 11, 1995, in an *Independent Journal* article, Michael Wornum, who sat as a BCDC commissioner while a Marin County supervisor and later served as a state assemblyman, was quoted as saying:

"BCDC has become extraordinarily bureaucratic and very negative and has been somewhat of a destructive element on any kind of change in the bay," he said. "On the other hand, I do think it fulfills a necessary function in controlling filling of the bay."

Wornum suggested the number of commissioners be cut from twenty-seven to twelve, half elected city and county officials and half appointed citizens.

"Most important, commissioners should have control over the staff, which has run rampant over the authority of the commission." Wornum said.

"The commission has not overturned a staff recommendation in a decade," he said.

"That makes a mockery of the public hearing," Wornum said.

Local jurisdictions already incorporate outside mandates in the rules they follow, such as the requirement for "affordable" housing, the announced expediency used to justify inclusion of the last boat owners at Waldo Point, who had originally refused berths, and, incidentally, how the drug problem was "solved" by changing its name to low income housing and subsidizing it. Marin County planners, for one, are perfectly competent to apply whatever rules they are handed. And think of the financial resources that can be diverted to sales, investment, production, and jobs instead of being spent on high priced suits endlessly talking to each other. Bay Area counties and cities would no doubt treat some applications differently than the BCDC might, but the differences would be small, reasonable, could always be challenged, and the bay would not suffer.

However, since the BCDC owns all the best current buzzwords and only a tiny fraction of the population of the Bay Area actually knows or has to deal with them, they are probably one bureaucracy that will be around forever. So much for wishful thinking.

Construction required to finish the project and formally accommodate the last boats in the Waldo Point Harbor commenced on Tuesday July 10, 2012, twenty-one days short of forty-three years in a planning process. Is that some kind of a record? Or, God help us all, is what we experienced the "new normal"?

Conclusion

I am deeply grateful to be a citizen of the United States and to be able to live under our Constitution. I admire the men who were able to put it together and the men and women who have protected it over the years. I don't respect those without honor, in or out of government, who work the system for their own benefit without consideration for others or a regard for the spirit of our founding law or a fundamental sense of fairness and fair play, as predictable as those things have always been in human affairs.

Government historically, as our Constitution makes so clear, that is, unrestrained, concentrated power, has always loomed as the natural enemy of individuals, either through commission or omission. The property owner and the residents at Waldo Point who tried to work within the law were subjected to a share of both. Most in positions of relevant governmental authority were simply unwilling to enforce the law equally against individuals who were part of an organized, loud, uncollectible group. They apparently wished to avoid being personally identified with multiple demonstrations, acts of violence and lawsuits by "the people," a political no-no. The rest of us, the other residents of Waldo Point Harbor, who incidentally are also people, can certainly understand politicians' and bureaucrats' distaste for such things because we endured years of it.

For good and bad, the name of the game is and always has been power. Acquiring power, using power, and retaining power, in whatever degree, has always been the objective—power to survive in a hostile environment, whether natural or man made, power to influence events, and the power to dictate to others. The extent to which restraints are placed on the concentration of power has always been the measure of a free people.

The genius of our Constitution is that it provides an arena, walled in by powerful checks and balances, where the ambitious and power-hungry, as well as the honorable and selfless, can duke it out in bloodless contests with the least possible permanent damage to the rest of us. Some of us forgot or ignored that intent big time in 1860 when the issue was slavery and periodically in lesser ways throughout our history.

Our Constitution works because it acknowledges human nature and accounts for it by embracing a philosophy that embodies a structure of law within which individuals and groups have the freedom to openly compete for their ideas and for power without the use of violence, the threat of violence, or the fear of violence. At Waldo Point, our government, at all levels, forgot or ignored that simplest to understand and most fundamental responsibility.

End

Endnotes

i   A. E. Housman, "Could Man Be Drunk Forever," version found at http://www.poemhunter.com/poem/could-man-be-drunk-forever/.

ii   From a release issued by the National Labor Relations Board describing an agreement it had reached with Teamsters Local 695.

iii   Correspondence obtained from Robert "Ducko" Rainey.

iv   Vidkun Quisling was head of the regime that collaborated with the Nazi occupation in Norway. The term is being used here as an adjective to describe "an evil collaborator."

CPSIA information can be obtained
at www.ICGtesting.com
Printed in the USA
FSHW011207190419
57410FS

9 781480 911031